Grow Your
Own Plants

Grow Your Own Plants

BOOKS

10 9 8 7 6 5 4 3 2 1

Published in 2013 by BBC Books, an imprint of
Ebury Publishing, a Random House Group Company

The Random House Group Limited Reg. No. 954009

Addresses for companies within the Random House
Group can be found at www.randomhouse.co.uk

The Random House Group Limited
supports The Forest Stewardship Council
(FSC®), the leading international forest
certification organisation. Our books
carrying the FSC label are printed on
FSC® certified paper. FSC is the only
forest certification scheme endorsed by
the leading environmental organisations,
including Greenpeace. Our paper
procurement policy can be found at
www.randomhouse.co.uk/environment

FSC
www.fsc.org
MIX
Paper from
responsible sources
FSC™ C004592

A CIP catalogue record for this book is available from
the British Library.

ISBN 978 1 84 990222 9

Produced by OutHouse!
Shalbourne, Marlborough, Wiltshire SN8 3QJ

BBC BOOKS
COMMISSIONING EDITOR: Lorna Russell
PROJECT EDITOR: Nicholas Payne
PRODUCTION: Rebecca Jones

OUTHOUSE!
COMMISSIONING EDITOR: Sue Gordon
SERIES EDITOR & PROJECT EDITOR: Polly Boyd
SERIES ART DIRECTOR: Robin Whitecross
CONTRIBUTING EDITOR: Richard Bird
DESIGNER: Louise Turpin
ILLUSTRATIONS by Lizzie Harper, Susan Hillier,
Janet Tanner
PHOTOGRAPHS by Jonathan Buckley except where
credited otherwise on page 96
CONCEPT DEVELOPMENT & SERIES DESIGN:
Elizabeth Mallard-Shaw, Sharon Cluett

Colour origination by Altaimage, London
Printed and bound by Firmengruppe APPL,
Wemding, Germany

Contents

Introduction

Gardening is one of the best and most fulfilling activities on earth, but it can sometimes seem complicated and confusing. The answers to problems can usually be found in books, but big fat gardening books can be rather daunting. Where do you start? How can you find just the information you want without wading through lots of stuff that is not appropriate to your particular problem? Well, a good index is helpful, but sometimes a smaller book devoted to one particular subject fits the bill better – especially if it is reasonably priced and if you have a small garden where you might not be able to fit in everything suggested in a larger volume.

The *How to Garden* books aim to fill that gap – even if sometimes it may be only a small one. They are clearly set out and written, I hope, in a straightforward, easy-to-understand style. I don't see any point in making gardening complicated, when much of it is based on common sense and observation. (All the key techniques are explained and illustrated, and I've included plenty of tips and tricks of the trade.)

There are suggestions on the best plants and the best varieties to grow in particular situations and for a particular effect. I've tried to keep the information crisp and to the point so that you can find what you need quickly and easily and then put your new-found knowledge into practice. Don't worry if you're not familiar with the Latin names of plants. They are there to make sure you can find the plant as it will be labelled in the nursery or garden centre, but where appropriate I have included common names, too. Forgetting a plant's name need not stand in your way when it comes to being able to grow it.

Above all, the *How to Garden* books are designed to fill you with passion and enthusiasm for your garden and all that its creation and care entails, from designing and planting it to maintaining it and enjoying it. For more than fifty years gardening has been my passion, and that initial enthusiasm for watching plants grow, for trying something new and for just being outside pottering has never faded. If anything I am keener on gardening now than I ever was and get more satisfaction from my plants every day. It's not that I am simply a romantic, but rather that I have learned to look for the good in gardens and in plants, and there is lots to be found. Oh, there are times when I fail – when my plants don't grow as well as they should and I need to try harder. But where would I rather be on a sunny day? Nowhere!

The *How to Garden* handbooks will, I hope, allow some of that enthusiasm – childish though it may be – to rub off on you, and the information they contain will, I hope, make you a better gardener, as well as opening your eyes to the magic of plants and flowers.

Introducing propagation

One of the most enjoyable and rewarding aspects of gardening is growing your own plants from scratch. Starting with a handful of seeds no bigger than a speck of dust, you can produce a bed packed with flowers or vegetables or even – given time – large specimen shrubs or trees. It enables you to produce a multitude of plants at little expense, reproducing favourites for your own garden or to share with others. Such creative powers are within the reach of any gardener. You don't need green fingers, no matter what people may say, and once you've experienced the wonder and excitement of this fulfilling pastime you'll never want to stop.

How plants grow

Plants have a strong survival instinct and will increase (reproduce) from seeds, bits of broken-off stem, underground runners or by dividing themselves, as you can see from the weeds that can quickly multiply throughout the garden. In order to understand how to increase plants in cultivation, it helps to know how plants grow and reproduce in nature, so you can provide the most favourable conditions and use the appropriate technique for the plant you want to propagate.

What plants need for growth

Plants need six key elements for survival: food, water, air, light, physical support (usually provided by soil) and sufficient warmth. The good gardener will ensure the plant has all six components, and will take care to get the balance right, especially when propagating, as young plants are considerably more vulnerable than established ones.

Nutrients and water

In nature, food is provided by nutrients in the soil, but when propagating plants it's best to provide a specially prepared compost, such as sowing compost or cutting compost, which holds the optimum amount of nutrients and composition for propagation (*see* pages 16–17).

Ample moisture is also extremely important. Some plants need more water than others, but few will tolerate drought conditions or being 'flooded'. Small seedlings are incapable of storing quantities of water and therefore need watering regularly. On the other hand, it's vital not to overwater them or they can easily become waterlogged, which can result in roots rotting and plants dying. (*See also* pages 18–19.)

Air and light

Like all growing things, plants need air, to provide essential oxygen and carbon dioxide and create the right kind of atmosphere for the plant to thrive. Too much humidity in the air and the plant becomes 'steamed up', like a window, which promotes the growth of diseases such as mildew, so it's important to provide sufficient ventilation around plants (*see* page 15). However, over-breezy conditions will dry out the leaves, causing wilting.

Plants will grow in very dark conditions – even in a cupboard – but they go in search of light and quickly become very long and drawn, and will be weak and sickly. Most plants need plenty of light to thrive, but when young they have to be kept away from full sunshine, as it will quickly shrivel them (this is especially true of woodland plants, which dislike bright conditions even when fully grown). A lightly shaded greenhouse or a windowsill out of direct sun is ideal for seedlings.

Soil and warmth

Garden soil provides support and anchorage for a plant's roots, and also contains the nutrients and moisture that most plants need. However, it is perfectly possible to

Water and nutrients in the soil are absorbed by the roots and carried up the stem to the leaves. The young shoot pushes up to the light and air.

grow many plants simply in water to which nutrients have been added; this soil-free method, known as hydroponics, is outside the scope of this book, although some more experienced gardeners might like to experiment with it.

Plants also need adequate warmth to grow (they stop growing when the temperature drops). As a general rule, most plants that are hardy in temperate Britain grow actively between temperatures of 7–30°C (45–86°F). Below or above that range, photosynthesis ceases and the plants are just 'ticking over'. Many plants we want to grow in our gardens need warmth for the seed to germinate (*see* box, page 14, and pages 27–8), and some require protection from frost or winter wet if they're to survive (*see* page 19).

Different propagation methods

There are numerous methods of propagation, but essentially they fall into two categories: by seed (sexual reproduction) or by vegetative (asexual) methods. The reason for choosing one propagation method over another is usually because it is the easiest or most reliable way of producing new plants. However, there is also another very important reason, and that is to enable the gardener to have a certain amount of control over the qualities of the resulting plants.

A wide range of plants are grown from cuttings taken from the shoots, leaves or roots of another plant. The offspring will invariably resemble its parent.

Hellebores (here, sown in modules) are easy to grow from seed, but named varieties are likely to differ from the parent plant.

Growing from seed

There are many advantages to growing from seed. However, the results aren't always predictable because of genetic variation. For instance, if you take seed from a tall red plant there is no guarantee it will come 'true', and the result might be a short plant with pink flowers. Part of the excitement of growing plants from seed is that you're never quite certain what you might get. Chances are it will be close to the original, but sometimes you get something quite new and original. For more on growing plants from seed, *see* pages 22–34.

Vegetative methods

Propagating by vegetative methods involves taking a part of the original plant and using it to produce new plants. There are various vegetative propagation methods, including taking cuttings, layering, division and grafting. Unlike growing from seed, vegetative methods always result in a plant that is genetically identical to its parent. For instance, if the parent is tall and has red flowers with yellow-variegated leaves, all the offspring will also have these properties. For more on vegetative propagation methods, *see* pages 36–65.

Tools and equipment

One of the great things about propagation is that you don't need much more equipment than a set of general garden tools (a spade, fork, rake and hoe). However, a few extra items will make the job quite a bit easier as well as increase your success rate. For example, it's surprising how many pots of seed will germinate quite happily if they're simply placed outdoors, but a heated propagator, greenhouse, or even a windowsill, will speed up the process and in some cases increase the number of seedlings produced.

Equipment for sowing seed and taking cuttings

There are several hand tools and other small items that are useful when sowing seeds, taking cuttings or propagating by other vegetative methods. You can buy them ready made, but many can be adapted from other tools or constructed from odd bits of wood or plastic. Don't feel you need all the items on the list all at once – start with the minimum and see what you need as you progress. For details on larger items and equipment needed once the cuttings have been prepared and for maintenance, *see* pages 13–15.

Garden knives and other cutters
A garden knife or other cutting tool is essential for taking and preparing cuttings. Garden knives come in all shapes and sizes. Whichever you choose, it must be kept very sharp with a sharpening stone, otherwise it will tear the base of the cutting, allowing disease in more readily. Alternatively, you can use a pair of sharp-pointed, stainless-steel scissors or a craft knife for lighter, softer stems and a good pair of secateurs for thicker, woodier ones.

Containers and compost
Essential equipment when propagating plants under cover (*see* pages 12 and 16–17).

Propagator
This will increase your chances of success with a range of seeds and is useful for raising cuttings (*see* pages 13–14).

Scoop
Some kind of container for transferring compost into pots and trays is essential. You can buy one ready made, or improvise – a flowerpot or a large polythene bottle cut to shape will work fine.

Dibber
Good for making planting holes for inserting cuttings, sowing seeds or pricking out seedlings. Alternatively, use the end of a pencil.

Sieve
Useful if you want to sift seeds, compost to cover seeds, or other organic material when making compost mixes. Specialized seed sieves are available, but domestic ones are fine, provided you don't use them for culinary purposes once they've been used for gardening!

Block of wood
Good for tamping down the compost in trays or pots. Ideally, use a rectangular or square shape for trays and a rounded form

Any cutting implements you use for propagation must be very sharp and clean to prevent ragged cuts (which increase the likelihood of diseases entering the plant).

for pots. They are easily made, or use the base of a flowerpot instead.

Garden line
A length of string held taut between two canes; useful when marking out drills if sowing direct into the garden (*see* page 33).

Plant labels
Essential in order to identify your pots of seeds, cuttings and seedlings (*see* box, page 12).

Watering can
Use a watering can with a fine rose to water newly sown seeds, seedlings and cuttings.

Sprayer
For misting young plants that need a humid atmosphere or for spraying with pesticide or fungicide if you have to. A small, hand-held sprayer is adequate; don't use the same sprayer for both tasks.

A selection of pots of different sizes and seed trays is indispensable for sowing seeds and raising cuttings.

Containers

Unless you're sowing outside in the open garden, the one thing you must have is a container to grow plants in. There are three main possibilities: pots, trays or modules.

One mistake that gardeners often make when they start propagating plants is to over-sow or take too many cuttings. If a whole packet of seed is spread over a tray it can produce literally hundreds of seedlings, and to pot all these up would cost a fortune in pots and compost. Unless you're selling plants or going in for mass bedding, you need only a handful of any one type of plant, so it's best to sow just a few seeds in a pot.

Whatever type of container you use, you'll need a cover. You can purchase specially made lids, but an inflated polythene bag will do, as long as it doesn't touch the plants.

Most containers can be recycled and used year after year, but it's vital to wash and dry them thoroughly.

Pots

A 9cm (3½in) pot is adequate for most purposes, but half-pans (which are wider) can also be useful for slightly larger quantities, and you'll need some bigger ones for potting on. Pots take up less space than a tray and are also usually deeper, which allows the roots of the seedlings to develop further. Plastic pots are better than those made of clay, as they don't dry out as quickly.

Trays

Trays are ideal for larger quantities of vegetables or bedding plants, or for root cuttings, which take up more space than other types of cutting. Trays come in two standard sizes – 'trays' and 'half-trays'. If possible, buy deep trays, as shallow ones dry out faster and don't allow sufficient space for root development, so the seedlings need pricking out sooner.

Modules

For mass production, modules (plastic trays with individual cells, *see* page 10) can be useful. These come in various shapes and sizes as well as materials.

The advantage of modules is that there is usually only one plant per cell, so when it comes to planting out the compost does not have to be broken up to remove each seedling, resulting in very little root disturbance and plants establishing more quickly. However, not all plants like modules and some individual cells are very small, so the seedlings need to be moved on as soon as possible. Since modules are often flimsy, if you're likely to need to move them frequently, place them inside a tray before sowing.

> ### Don't forget
>
> Some containers are made of organic material, such as paper or fibre, through which roots can grow, and you can plant out the whole thing, pot and all. You can also make improvised pots from recycling household items, such as the insides of toilet rolls.

> ### Don't forget
>
> When writing a plant label, always start the name at the top of the label and write towards the point. If you do it the other way round, the most important part of the name is likely to be buried in the soil and you'll have to remove the label each time to read it.

Labelling and keeping records

One pot of seed looks exactly like another and confusion can easily occur if you rely on memory, so make sure you label all newly propagated plants. As well as the name of the plant, you'll need to include the date of sowing or taking the cutting and the source.

Other records, either written in a notebook or on a computer, can be useful if you have the kind of methodical, tidy mind that will keep them up to date. A lot can be learnt from keeping details of temperatures and the compost used, how long it took for seeds to germinate and cuttings to root, whether mist or heat was used and many other details. All this will add to your knowledge and ability.

The propagating environment

The ideal environment for propagation depends on the type of plant and method of propagation – some need little care, and are happy simply placed on a bright windowsill in the home, while others require carefully regulated conditions. There are various pieces of equipment that help to provide the ideal environment, enabling the propagated material to survive and establish as a young plant. Again, don't feel you need to rush out and buy all the equipment straight away – keep it simple to start with, then, once the propagating bug has got you firmly in its grip, you may want to think of other items that will either increase your efficiency or make things easier.

Seedlings benefit from the protected environment provided by a basic propagator with a rigid plastic lid.

Propagators

A propagator creates an enclosed, protected, humid atmosphere, which is good for the germination of seed and for keeping cuttings alive while they produce roots. Propagators range from a simple polythene bag slipped over a pot or an old plastic food container to a state-of-the-art piece of equipment with built-in heating and mist units. The one that many growers choose is a combined tray and transparent plastic lid (*see* above right). Once the seed has germinated and the cuttings have rooted, more air is needed to prevent the young plants rotting off, so all good propagators have vents that can be opened.

Some seeds benefit from heat and most cuttings root more easily with

Soil-warming cables and propagating frames

When you see soil-warming cables at the local garden centre or on a gardening website, you might dismiss them as being for more experienced gardeners. In fact, they are easy to set up and use. As their name implies, soil-warming cables are intended to warm soil, and their usual use is to create a heated propagating frame (*see* right), but you can also use them above ground to warm the air. It is easy to rig up a system that will keep a small area frost free, which is more economical than heating the air in the whole greenhouse. For example, you can bring a lightweight, portable cold frame into the greenhouse and position it over cables buried in sand. Add some polystyrene insulation boards around the sides, and you have a snug home for your more tender young plants.

The main use of soil-warming cables is to enable you to make a heated propagating frame that exactly suits your needs. You create a frame, bury the cable in a layer of sand and then either insert pots of cuttings and seeds on the surface or insert your cuttings into a layer of compost on top of the sand. A thermostat enables you to control the temperature and prevents plants overheating in warm weather.

HOW TO MAKE A PROPAGATING FRAME

You can make the frame almost any size, but bear in mind that you may want to cover it with a lid. Also, make sure it is not too big or too heavy for your greenhouse shelves. The third factor to consider is power. A propagating frame in an unheated greenhouse needs about 10 watts per 30cm (12in) square; in a heated greenhouse 7.5 watts per 30cm (12in) square is adequate. The length of the cable determines the wattage. A frame of 90 x 75cm (3 x 2½ft) in an unheated greenhouse needs a 6m (20ft) cable delivering 75 watts. This should suit the average gardener. A frame measuring 75cm x 2m (2½ x 6ft) would need a 12m (40ft) cable delivering 150 watts. If you want additional heat, use a deeper box and run a second cable with a separate thermostat around the sides.

① Make a box from wood: around 15cm (6in) deep is ideal; alternatively, buy an aluminium plunge tray. If a wooden frame is used, it is a good idea to protect the base with a sheet of polythene.

② Spread a 5cm (2in) layer of coarse horticultural grit and then about 2.5cm (1in)

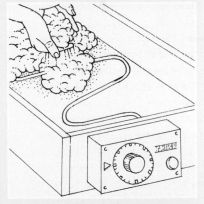

of coarse sand. Lay the soil-warming cable in loops that don't touch on top of the sand, covering as big an area as possible. To make the cable more pliable, switch it on to warm up for a few minutes beforehand.

③ Cover the cable with a 2.5cm (1in) layer of coarse sand and attach a thermostat to the cable. Make sure the sand is always damp when the frame is in use.

A greenhouse makes an excellent plant nursery, where you can sow seeds, raise cuttings and generally manage and increase your stock of plants.

warmth, so committed gardeners often invest in propagators with heating elements in them.

A wide selection of ready-made heated electric propagators is available in garden centres or online. There are two main types: fixed-temperature and thermostatically controlled. The fixed-temperature variety provides heat at about 19°C (66°F), which is ideal for germinating a range of seeds. A thermostatically controlled propagator enables you to control the temperature, which has many advantages.

Other possibilities include buying a soil-warming cable and/or making a propagator (*see* box, page 13).

Greenhouses and potting sheds

A greenhouse is of great benefit, not only to the plants but also to the gardener, as it is usually a pleasant place in which to work, especially when it is cold outdoors. Another advantage is that it is usually equipped with benches or work surfaces, so you can work at a comfortable height. The greenhouse need not be heated, although if you're growing tender plants this may be a necessity.

Mini-greenhouses, made of glass or polythene, are useful in confined spaces. They need some sun, so ideally position them against a

south-facing wall, which will also provide warmth. Since they're small they can heat up rapidly to high temperatures – provide ventilation by opening the door on sunny days; you might need to add shading too, even quite early in the season. Mini-greenhouses can also be used inside a normal cold greenhouse to give extra protection or used in lieu of a propagator for providing cuttings or pots of seed with an enclosed atmosphere.

A potting shed is a luxury, but is well worth having if you become a keen propagator. It's ideal for storing pots, composts and tools and provides a good working environment. However, unlike a greenhouse most sheds aren't light enough for plants to thrive.

Humidity and heat

Providing heat to help the germination of seed or the rooting of cuttings can be a vexed question. Many gardeners propagate very successfully without the use of any heat at all, yet others swear by it. Either way, heat will often speed up germination and the rooting of cuttings. Humidity is also important. In the home, a kitchen or bathroom windowsill can often provide a sufficiently moist atmosphere for plants; alternatively, you could install a misting unit in the greenhouse (*see* opposite).

Most perennials come from temperate climates and germinate without heat in the wild and therefore will do so in the garden. On the other hand, a lot of annuals come from warmer climates and germinate only once the temperature begins to rise in spring, and it is this temperature you need to provide. Commercial seed merchants often give optimum temperatures for germinating seed. The difficulty here is that it is impossible to have various types of seed all germinating at different temperatures; also, different merchants often give different temperatures, so these should be taken only as a guide. A gentle heat is usually sufficient.

Opening roof vents instantly increases airflow and reduces the temperature within the greenhouse.

Ventilation and shading

An adequate supply of gently moving air is vital in the greenhouse to prevent seedlings 'damping off' (rotting). In a cool greenhouse, this means opening windows, but in an enclosed, heated greenhouse you'll need to install a fan. You could fit automatic window openers, which will increase ventilation as the greenhouse warms up.

Too much sun and heat can result in shrivelled, scorched seedlings, and at the height of summer it is often necessary to reduce the amount of light coming into the greenhouse. Depending on weather conditions, you may require shading from late spring until early autumn. There are three main options for providing shade: using shade paints or adding mesh or net shades or roller blinds. Automatic blinds are another refinement that some propagators use: in hot, sunny weather they close, to prevent the sun scorching the seedlings, but open when it's overcast, allowing maximum light to reach the plants.

Automatic watering systems

A commercial technique that is now in widespread use among amateur growers is the use of automatic watering equipment. This is particularly useful for people who are away during the day at work, especially in hot weather, as pots may need watering several times, particularly if they're under glass. It is also useful if you're on holiday and don't have anyone to water all your much-loved plants.

There are three different types of equipment available. A trickle system (*see* right) supplies water to individual pots through tubes. Another method is capillary matting on which the pots or trays stand (*see* bottom right). The third, much more costly, piece of equipment is an overhead sprinkler, which can be used in conjunction with a mist unit.

Mist units

A mist unit is used to keep cuttings moist without drowning them, by spraying them with a very fine mist. This helps prevent the foliage from drying out and wilting, coaxing even the most reluctant cuttings into growth. The constant water flow also discourages fungal infections.

Small units can be purchased by the home-grower, although it is also possible to buy units that will keep whole benches or even the whole greenhouse sprayed. These units have an artificial 'leaf', which detects when the cuttings are beginning to dry out and switches the mister on.

Watering systems

There comes a time when doing all your watering by hand can seem a bit of a chore. Fortunately, there are many ways to reduce the workload.

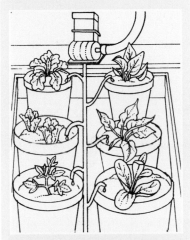

Trickle systems work by attaching a flexible hose to a tap with a timer on it. Narrow tubes linked to the hose can be fed into pots and containers. When the tap is on, water is delivered to the pots in a steady flow. Different heads drip or shower water onto the soil; some are even mini-spikes pushed into the soil.

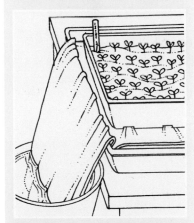

If you don't have a tap in or near the greenhouse, capillary matting can be very useful. Spread the matting over a waterproof tray and dangle the end in a bucket of water. Put pots or trays of plants on top of the matting. It absorbs water from the bucket and the plants absorb water from it.

Growing mediums

When propagating plants under cover, the appropriate growing medium is vital for success. Always use fresh, sterile compost rather than garden soil or compost from your compost heap, as it is light and well aerated and less likely to harbour pests and diseases. Gardening friends may suggest all kinds of 'magic mixes' that they use to propagate plants, such as cows' urine or ox blood, but for the beginner it's best to stick to more tried-and-tested recipes specially formulated for propagation. (For sowing seed direct into the ground, *see* pages 32–4.)

Ready-made composts

If you're new to propagating, it's probably best to buy a ready-made compost, but as your confidence increases you can experiment with your own mixes (*see* opposite).

When moving a seedling from a tray or module to a pot of its own, it's best to use a balanced potting compost, such as John Innes No. 1.

Seed composts

Most seed composts are moisture-retentive yet free-draining and low in nutrients (because too rich a compost can 'burn' the seedlings' roots). There are two main types of ready-made seed compost: loam-based (also known as soil-based) or loamless (soilless). Loam-based composts usually contain sterilized loam, peat (or peat substitute) and sand and are heavier and freer-draining than loamless types, making it easier to control moisture content. The organic-based ones are lighter and retain moisture better, but this can make them wetter and more difficult to re-wet if they dry out completely. There are arguments for and against, and ultimately it comes down to personal preference.

Cutting composts

Like young seedlings, cuttings do not need many nutrients until roots have formed. Special cutting composts have been devised which provide good drainage and physical support for the plant. These are often only a 50/50 mixture of sharp sand (or vermiculite or perlite, *see* opposite) and an organic material. Increasingly, commercial manufacturers of loamless composts are combining both seed and cutting compost into one composition. Try out various brands and choose the one that you think works best for you and your plants.

Potting composts

Once your seedlings have germinated or cuttings taken root, they should be potted up (*see* page 20) into a richer compost and gradually moved on to an even richer medium. Loam-based composts are usually composed to a formula devised by the John Innes Institute and are numbered 1 to 3 (often abbreviated to JIP1, JIP2 and JIP3), each increasing in the quantity of added nutrients.

Specialist composts

The composts mentioned on these pages work for most plants, but there are some that need a specialist compost. For example, acid-loving plants, such as rhododendrons, heathers and camellias, require an ericaceous compost, which contains no lime. Orchids also prefer a specially formulated compost. Alpines need extra sharp sand added for faster drainage. Bulbs are often grown in 'bulb fibre', but this isn't really necessary for propagating purposes and ordinary composts will do just as well. Specialist composts can all be made easily by the gardener and are likely to be covered in specialist plant books.

Loamless multipurpose composts

Originally, loamless multipurpose composts were formulated to be suitable for seed-sowing, taking cuttings, potting and final potting. Today, with the reduction in use of peat and increasing availability of alternatives such as green waste and wood fibre in composts, many so-called multipurpose composts do not give good results for seed-sowing and rooting cuttings. So always check the manufacturer's recommendations before use, and if in doubt use a specifically formulated compost.

John Innes No. 1 This is used for pricking out (*see* page 29) or potting up young seedlings or rooted cuttings and has a balanced nutrient content to suit most young plants.

John Innes No. 2 A multipurpose mix for general potting of most established plants into medium-size pots. Contains double the amount of nutrient found in John Innes No. 1.

John Innes No. 3 A richer mixture for final repotting of hungry vegetable plants and for permanent container plantings of mature foliage plants and shrubs, all of which benefit from the added nutrients.

Some plant types, including acid-loving plants such as rhododendrons and camellias, require a specialist potting compost (*see* box, opposite).

Homemade composts

If you get really interested in propagation, you can create your own composts. Making your own isn't at all difficult and has a lot to recommend it – you can experiment with mixes and find the one that is most suitable for your plants.

Using sterilized soil

You can use your own garden soil as a base for compost mixes, provided it's sufficiently moist, well drained and reasonably fertile. However, it must first be sterilized to kill off harmful organisms that may affect your seedlings or cuttings during propagation – although your plants may grow happily in the open ground, if you're raising young

Organic matter can be used to create your own potting composts; avoid peat for conservation reasons.

plants in pots in warmer conditions, weed seeds spring into life and spores and micro-organisms can multiply to a harmful level. If you want to use your own soil, you'll

need to invest in an electric soil-sterilizing unit, which heats the soil to a certain temperature and kills off pests and diseases; they're not cheap, but if you're really keen it will be worth it in the long run. Alternatively, you can buy bags (or lorry-loads) of pre-sterilized soil.

Other ingredients

In the past, materials used to make composts were limited mainly to loam, sharp sand and peat. Now there are ethical problems with peat, so the peat is often substituted with a more environmentally friendly material such as coir (coconut fibre) or well-rotted leaf mould, which you can make yourself by putting dead leaves in perforated black polythene bags in autumn to rot down for using the following year. The leaf mould needs to be really well rotted, and is best for larger, more robust seeds, such as runner beans, rather than smaller, more delicate plants.

Perlite and vermiculite are artificial materials that are now widely used as a substitute for horticultural grit (*see* page 27).

Compost recipes

Below are some basic recipes for compost mixes for propagation, but you can adapt these to obtain the ideal medium for individual plants. Later, as the plants become more established, you'll need to move the plants on to a richer potting compost (*see* opposite).

LOAM-BASED SEED COMPOST
- 1 part loam (good soil), sterilized
- 2 parts sharp sand
- 2 parts sieved organic material such as coir or other peat substitute
- 1.2kg (2½lb) superphosphate plus 600g (1¼lb) ground limestone for every cubic metre (35 cubic feet) of compost

LOAMLESS SEED COMPOST
- 3 parts sieved organic material such as

coir or other peat substitute
- 1 part sharp sand
- 1.2kg (2½lb) superphosphate plus 600g (1¼lb) ground limestone for every cubic metre (35 cubic feet) of compost

CUTTING COMPOST
- 1 part sharp sand (alternatively, vermiculite or perlite)
- 1 part peat substitute (alternatively, one part general multipurpose compost)

Care and maintenance

In the wild, where there is no one to look after a seedling once it has germinated, many plants produce hundreds of seedlings in the hope that at least one will survive. In the garden, where each seedling is precious, especially if it is seed from a rare or difficult plant, we do our best to make certain that as many survive as possible by providing appropriate care and maintenance.

Eliminating weeds

One of the key ways to increase a seedling's chances of survival is to ensure that there is no competition from other plants, especially vigorous ones. Whether a seedling is growing in a container or in the open garden, try to keep the compost or surrounding soil weed-free. This not only reduces the competition for nutrients and water, but it also helps with the prevention of diseases. A thick mat of weeds around seedlings reduces air circulation and encourages fungal diseases. Likewise, certain weeds are likely to be host to diseases that can spread to the neighbouring seedlings. For example, ragwort is often covered with fungal rust.

Critical times

There are two critical times for young plants in pots. The first is during hot weather, when they can dry out very quickly. It is essential to check them several times a day under such conditions. The second is when you're away on holiday – you can't just abandon them to their own devices and hope all will be well on your return. If you're away from the home for substantial periods of time, it's well worth setting up an automatic watering system (see page 15), or asking a neighbour to pop in regularly to water and keep an eye on your plants.

Watering

Seedlings grown under glass are very dependent on the gardener, as they must be watered and fed. This is not as straightforward as it seems, and providing the right amount of water is crucial – too little and the seedlings will dry out, too much and you'll swamp them; remember, seedlings usually have relatively small root systems, so they can't take up as much water as mature plants. Check the soil in the pots with your fingers and keep it just moist without being waterlogged.

If sowing seed direct into the garden, you need to water straight after sowing, and the seedlings when they first emerge, but once the plants have become established,

Don't forget

When watering seedlings, always use a fine rose turned upwards to create a light spray and avoid disturbing the compost. Start watering at the edge of the tray or pot and work steadily across to ensure even distribution.

Make sure you regularly water plants grown in the greenhouse or in pots, particularly in hot weather.

with the roots growing deep into the soil, it should no longer be necessary to water. Vegetables usually require watering in dry weather, but most flowering plants, except those in containers, will tolerate a considerable amount of drought and it is not necessary to water them regularly.

Practising good hygiene

Propagating plants is very enjoyable, and you don't want to view it as a chore. However, it's worth bearing in mind that taking a few basic precautions will go a long way in helping your new plants get away to a healthy start and give you the best possible chance of success.

■ Never introduce a plant into the greenhouse that has a disease or pest on it. If in doubt about the origins of a plant, remove it from its pot and replace all the soil with fresh compost that you know is disease- and pest-free.

■ Good tool hygiene is very important, especially where blades will be in direct contact with cut surfaces. It's best to sterilize tools before use by dipping them into surgical spirit or methylated spirits; this will also help to remove any build-up of resin or sap from the plants. Sterilizing tools is imperative if you've been cutting any plant material that you know to have been diseased.

■ Unless you're using new pots and trays, clean all containers thoroughly before use, removing any loose material, and wash them with warm, soapy water. You can still find special brushes with a tapering shape, designed for scrubbing pots, although any brush will do.

■ It's surprising how often little drifts of detritus, such as dead leaves, can pile up in corners of the greenhouse. Always try to remove dead plants or parts of plants as soon as possible rather than leaving them lying around, as they can harbour pests and diseases.

■ Once or twice a year, give the greenhouse a really good clear-out. Autumn is often recommended and means you get rid of pests that may otherwise overwinter in the warmer environment. Alternatively, early spring is a good time. Clean the shelves and staging with warm, soapy water, remove the debris, and wash and clean the glass and framework.

Feeding

Newly germinated seedlings and rooted cuttings need hardly any food – there should be enough in the compost – but as they grow and are potted on (*see* page 20), they will require more. However, be very careful not to overdo it. Too rich a diet can damage the roots and create overblown plants, making them more prone to diseases.

There are plenty of proprietary brands of plant feed to choose from. Some are sprinkled on top of the compost, while others are dissolved in water and then watered in. Slow-release fertilizers are in many ways the best, as the granules slowly, sometimes over months, release the food, saving you having to remember to feed. Follow the instructions on the label as to frequency and quantity of feeding, because these vary depending on the manufacturer.

Pinching out

Many plants that bush out, such as dianthus and sweet peas (shown above), as opposed to growing from a single stem, can benefit from having their main growing-tip removed, as this encourages them to branch out, forming a good, rounded specimen.

Scrubbing pots can seem like a chore, but it is important to ensure the containers don't harbour any pests and diseases from the previous year.

Winter protection

There is no need to heat the greenhouse over winter unless it contains tender plants. In colder weather, it is usually sufficient to cover the plants with a few layers of horticultural fleece. On the other hand, some warmth should be introduced if there is the likelihood of a prolonged spell of very cold weather, as under these circumstances the compost may well freeze solid and kill the roots.

Thermostatically controlled electric heaters are the most convenient, although paraffin heaters are also popular. However, the latter introduce a lot of water vapour into the atmosphere, which can encourage fungal diseases.

Many plants, especially hardy perennials and woody subjects, can be increased from seed sown in pots and then left in a sheltered place in the open – there is no need for a greenhouse. These will tolerate the cold weather, and often appreciate it, as it helps break dormancy (*see* page 25), but they can be less happy about a wet winter. Lack of hardiness for many plants has more to do with being over-wet than too cold. So for wet, winter months it is often a good idea to put pots in a cold frame or cover them with a cloche or basic frame covered with polythene. Make sure air is allowed to circulate by keeping the doors or sides partially open, and if making a polythene frame, construct a sloping 'lid' so that water easily runs off it.

Hardening off

You should avoid moving plants direct from a greenhouse (especially if it is heated) into their beds outside. The seedlings will have difficulty adjusting and at best will take a while to recover and start growing away; worse, they will remain stunted or even die.

If you have a cold frame (*see* page 42), put the plants that are ready to be planted out in it and then, over the next couple of weeks, open the frames a bit more each day. At first, shut them at night and on cold, wet days, but after a fortnight or so you can start leaving them open. If you don't have a cold frame, take the pots outside for longer periods each day and eventually nights too, covering them with horticultural fleece on their first few nights out. Once they've hardened off, they're ready to be planted.

Potting on

When you first prick out seedlings (*see* page 29) or pot up cuttings (*see* page 42), you'll need to plant them into a fairly small pot; if the container is too large, the small roots won't be able to take up all the available moisture and so the compost is likely to remain sodden, potentially causing rot. However, as the plant grows you'll need to transfer it into a larger pot (known as 'potting on'), or the seedling will become stunted. Pot it up one size each time (pots tend to increase in increments of 3cm/1¼in). You'll also need to provide plants with a richer compost as they grow larger (*see* pages 16–17).

Plants grown under cover need gradual acclimatization (hardening off) if they are to survive outdoors.

In the case of most seedlings and cuttings, if diseases or pests get a firm hold there is little chance of cure, as the plants are too small to have any reserve of strength to allow recovery. Try to prevent problems from occurring in the first place by providing optimum conditions for growth and keeping plants healthy. A vigorous young plant stands a much better chance of becoming a first-class mature specimen than one that is struggling.

Many insects and their larvae are very welcome in the garden as they eat pests.
① Ladybirds and their larvae devour large numbers of aphids.
② Hoverfly larvae also feed on aphids.

Cultivation problems

Many more young plants die from lack of water than from pests and diseases. When a plant becomes dehydrated, its growth will be stunted and it will also be more prone to health problems. A sure sign of dehydration is when the leaves start to wilt; when this is the case, you'll need to water straightaway. Beware of overwatering, as this can also cause problems (see pages 18–19).

Shortage of light and too much sun also spell big trouble for plants. Dim conditions will lead to a plant turning 'leggy' as it leans and stretches towards the light, and it won't thrive. Conversely, too much sun is likely to shrivel the leaves, which will kill plants. Another problem with sunlight is that drops of water on the leaves may act as a magnifying glass, intensifying the sun's rays and leaving scorch marks on the foliage.

Preventing diseases

The commonest disease that takes hold of young plants is damping off (see right). Here the 'neck' of the seedling or cutting becomes infected with a fungal disease and rots. There are several ways of preventing this. Sow seeds thinly in good-quality compost; a layer of horticultural grit on the surface aids drainage, so the neck doesn't sit in water. Good hygiene, ventilation and plenty of light are also vital. As a preventative measure, water seedlings with a copper-based fungicide; once the seedling is infected, it's too late.

Coping with common pests

One of the commonest pests is the aphid, also known as greenfly. Be vigilant and catch them early, before populations build up. On bigger plants, it's relatively easy to control them by squeezing them between finger and thumb, but this isn't so simple with small, delicate seedlings or cuttings. You may need to spray the insects with a suitable pesticide as soon as you see any. Organic controls are available. As with many other pest problems, encouraging predators such as ladybirds, lacewings and hoverflies is helpful (see top right), and you could also consider using a biological control for greenhouse plants.

The other main pest of the greenhouse is the red spider mite (see below), which causes the leaves to go dull and then yellow as the mites feed on the sap. The leaves will be covered with a fine webbing that protects the breeding colonies. Good hygiene and maintaining high humidity in the greenhouse (for instance, by 'damping down', or watering surfaces inside) will help to prevent this. If there is an infestation, various chemical and biological controls are available.

It is helpful to recognize plant problems and to try to avoid them.
① Damping off can kill seedlings.
② Red spider mite is debilitating and disfiguring and will stunt growth.

> ### Don't forget
>
> If you do start having real problems with propagation, cut your losses and start again, having first thoroughly cleaned and sterilized the location and equipment (see page 19).

Growing from seed

All creative activities are satisfying, but there's nothing quite like the buzz you get from turning a packet of seed into a border full of plants. If you're apprehensive about your ability, remember that in the wild nature does it without any help. Start with packets of familiar, tried-and-tested annuals or vegetables, and over time you'll develop the confidence to tackle more 'difficult' plants. Many so-called tricky plants are actually easy to grow once the gardener has a little extra knowledge and experience.

Sourcing, collecting and storing seed

When you first start gardening, your experience of growing plants generally tends to be limited to what's available in your local garden centre. Gradually, you'll discover that there is a vast world of opportunities out there, allowing you to grow rare and interesting plants that you didn't know existed.

Sourcing seed

Commercial seed is widely available, and most garden centres and small nurseries offer a great variety, usually enough to satisfy most gardeners. Alternatively, you can order seed direct from a catalogue. All the major seed merchants have a mail-order service, and the catalogues usually provide a greater variety than you'll see in the shops. One of life's great pleasures is to settle down on a winter's night with a pile of catalogues choosing next year's plants.

Garden societies

As their interest develops, many gardeners start visiting other gardens and joining local garden societies, and soon begin to discover the incredible diversity and abundance of plants available. Many garden clubs offer seed that has been collected by members to other members, either for a small sum or for free.

There are many benefits of joining a gardening society – having access to unusual seeds is one of them – but you need to be aware that the plant you end up with may not resemble the parent, because most of the seed comes from plants that are open pollinated; in other words, pollinated by bees that simply flit from one plant to another. Some species, such as columbines (*Aquilegia*), are very promiscuous and the cross-pollination can result in seed that is not 'true' to the seed parent; thus, a red aquilegia may produce blue offspring. On the whole, though, it's well worth taking the risk, and sometimes the resulting hybrid can be a stunning newcomer that will be the envy of your friends.

Some societies specialize in particular groups of plants (*see* box, left). For more general collections of seed, organizations such as the Royal Horticultural Society (RHS) also supply seed to members.

Seeds range in size, from tiny specks you can barely see to a coconut. They also vary greatly in shape.

Seed collectors

One little-known group of suppliers are the seed collectors. If you check specialist magazines, you will often see adverts with seed for sale from seed-collecting expeditions to remote parts of the world. This can become an exciting way of getting new and unusual plants. It is often possible to swap excess plants grown from this source with other enthusiasts, thus extending your collection of plants even further.

Planning what you're going to grow is half the fun of gardening, but beware: it's easy to get carried away!

Specialist societies

If you become interested in particular groups of plants, it's time to explore the specialist societies. As a member, you'll be able to gain greater knowledge from other enthusiasts, and will have the chance to obtain more unusual seeds. For example, there are relatively few different types of rock garden plants offered by commercial seed companies, but the Alpine Garden Society offers several thousand to its members, as does the Scottish Rock Garden Club and the American Rock Garden Society. Similarly, the Lily Group of the Royal Horticultural Society and the Cyclamen Society offer a magnificent range of seed in their own specialist areas. There are organizations for most specialist groups of plants.

Don't forget

When buying seed at a garden centre or nursery, check the use-by date on the packet and never buy old stock. Also, avoid packets that are exposed to full sunlight, as this may well have ruined the seed.

Collecting seed

It's always satisfying to collect seed from your own plants and increase your stock, either for your own use or to give away to fellow gardeners.

To collect seed, leave seedheads on the plants to mature and dry, and wait for a dry day. When the seedpods turn yellow or brown, break them open to extract the seeds and put them in a paper bag or an envelope. If the seeds don't come out easily, pick the whole stem and pop it into the bag (*see* below). You can either shake the seeds out of their pods, leave the bag open in a cool, dry place to allow the seed to dry out, or seal the bag and hang it up (*see* top right). Never use polythene bags, as they're likely to cause rot.

Once the seed is dry, remove the contents of the bag and clean the seed of creepy-crawlies, grit and

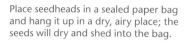
Place seedheads in a sealed paper bag and hang it up in a dry, airy place; the seeds will dry and shed into the bag.

chaff that may have been collected with it.

Some plants, for example geraniums, have an explosive seed dispersal system that flings the seed a long way from the plant and it is difficult to collect. Where this is the

case, put a paper or muslin bag over the unripe seedhead and tie it round the stem – you can then collect the seed from the bag.

Seed contained within fleshy fruit, such as hawthorns (*Crataegus*), roses (*Rosa*), rowans (*Sorbus*) and elder (*Sambucus*), needs to be removed before storing. The surest way is to pick the flesh off by hand; you may need to soak it first in warm water to soften it. Alternatively, put it in a sieve and rub hard so the flesh comes off.

Storing and using seed

Whether you've bought or collected your seed, always store it in a cool, dry place in labelled envelopes, dark jars or bottles or film canisters until it is required. Some gardeners like to keep it in the fridge.

Certain seed requires sowing as soon as you get it. The main plants that need to be sown fresh are those in the Ranunculaceae family, which includes buttercups (*Ranunculus*), hellebores, anemones, delphiniums, clematis and others.

Do not expect seed to remain viable for ever. While some will last up to three years or more given the right storage conditions, some of the larger, fleshy seeds lose energy faster and must be sown within the year.

Lychnis coronaria is fairly easy to propagate from seed. Cut the stems and shake the seeds into a paper bag.

Dormancy

Some seed, especially from trees and shrubs, exhibits a form of dormancy – a state that prevents it from germinating until the conditions are right for growth. If you're planning to propagate certain plants, it's vital to understand the process of dormancy or you may wonder why your pots of seed aren't sprouting.

In the wild, many seeds need a prolonged cold spell before they will germinate – this is nature's way of ensuring that they don't sprout too soon (in autumn, say), only to fall victim to harsh winter conditions; once the winter chill is over, it is spring and therefore safe to burst into life. Similarly, some seeds need a wet spell to penetrate their hard cases, signifying the 'rains' have arrived and there is sufficient moisture for the seedlings to survive. When propagating plants, you can mimic the conditions in the wild to encourage germination.

Seeds for cold treatment

The seed of many trees and shrubs, but also those of some herbaceous plants such as hellebores and certain primulas and lilies, will germinate faster if they're subjected to periods of cold (a process known as 'stratification'). You can allow this to happen naturally, by sowing the seed in autumn in pots and placing these outside over winter, allowing frost to break the dormancy. However, the problem with this method is that in some winters we don't have enough frost and it can take several winters before the seed decides it is time to germinate. To overcome this, many gardeners keep such seed in the fridge before sowing. Mix the seeds with a little damp compost in a plastic bag or box and put them in the fridge for a few weeks (up to three months at the most), then sow as normal. This cold treatment should speed up germination.

Seeds with hard cases

Some seeds have hard outer cases that need to be penetrated by cutting or scratching (a process known as 'scarifying') before they can germinate, to allow moisture in. With large seeds, it's best to use a sharp knife to nick the seed coat (this is known as 'chipping').

Some seeds have special requirements.
① Daphne (here, *D. bholua* 'Jacqueline Postill') needs a winter chill.
② Sweet peas benefit from scarifying.
③ *Cyclamen coum* seed germinates faster if soaked in water.

With smaller seeds, you can either rub them on abrasive paper or use a small file, or put the seed in a bag or container filled with grit or sand, or lined with coarse sandpaper, and give it a good, long shake.

Certain seeds are best soaked prior to sowing, usually in cold water, but sometimes (for instance, with *Passiflora*) warm water is recommended.

In the case of sweet peas (*Lathyrus*), you can get away with simply sowing the seed in the normal way without any pre-treatment, but germination will be faster and more reliable if you scarify the seed. Alternatively, some gardeners find that soaking the seed in warm water is enough.

Encouraging germination

Seed from the following plants is ideally treated before sowing to speed up the germination process.

COLD TREATMENT

Acer
Daphne
Euonymus
Fraxinus
Helleborus
Lewisia
Lilium (some)
Primula (some)
Sorbus

SCARIFYING

Cytisus
Genista
Lathyrus (many)
Lupinus
Paeonia

SOAKING

Acacia
Camellia
Canna
Cyclamen
Ipomoea
Lathyrus
Passiflora
Pittosporum

Sowing in pots, trays and modules

The advantage of sowing seed into containers is that plants are considerably easier to look after than those sown direct into the garden. The vagaries of the weather, as well as birds and slugs, can take their toll, whereas growing under cover means that you can keep a good eye on the young plants, and by the time they're put out into the wider world they've grown into sturdy specimens that can look after themselves.

You can sow seed into pots, trays or modules (*see* page 12); the method of sowing and tending is basically the same. For the best chances of germination, use fresh seed

Placing individual pots in larger trays without holes makes watering easier. Pour a few centimetres of water into the tray and it will seep up through the compost.

wherever possible. However, many seeds can last for a few seasons if they're stored properly (*see* page 24), and remember some need to be chilled, soaked or scarified before sowing (*see* page 25).

Preparing the compost
Take a clean pot and fill it to the rim with seed compost. Tap it on the bench and you'll find that the compost settles a little and also levels off in the pot.
   Next, take a circular block of wood the same size as the pot and

gently firm down the compost so that the surface is level with the lower edge of the pot. Alternatively, you can use the base of another clean pot to do the same thing. Do not press down too hard – water will not spread evenly through or be absorbed into compacted compost.

Sowing seed
In the case of large seeds, pick them up individually and push them into the compost, spacing each at some distance from its neighbours to ensure that each seedling will get its share of nutrients and moisture without too much competition. In a 9cm (3½in) pot or modules, you may sow just one or two seeds per pot. If you're growing something really big, such as a chestnut or

In the case of large seeds, sow one or two per pot. If both germinate, pull out and discard the weaker one.

Don't forget
The surface of the compost must be level before sowing. A sloping surface will result in uneven moisture distribution and all the seed being washed down to one side.

walnut, or even a vast avocado seed (yes, you can grow them from a supermarket fruit and they make a good house plant), put just one in each pot.

Small seeds should be scattered thinly over the surface of the compost as evenly as possible. There is often the temptation to use the whole packet, but if you do all the seedlings will be overcrowded and starved of both nutrients and light.

Cover the seeds in compost, ideally sieved, or in horticultural grit (*see* box, right). Larger seeds need a good covering, while small seeds need only a thin layer (for very fine seeds, *see* bottom right). Some seeds, such as *Eccremocarpus*, *Primula*, *Gentiana* and *Impatiens*, need full light to germinate, so leave them uncovered.

Stand the pots in a container of water (*see* opposite), so the plants will be watered from below. Remember to label the pots and/or trays or modules.

Germination

Place the seeds in a suitable location for germination. Bottom heat will help most seeds to germinate more quickly (18–21°C/65–70°F suits most plants), so use a heated propagator if you have one (*see* pages 13–14). If not, put them in an unheated propagator or cover trays or pots with a sheet of glass or clear acrylic, or a polythene bag (*see* page 28), and place them in a bright, sheltered part of the greenhouse or on a sunny windowsill. If the seeds need darkness, cover them with sheets of newspaper or a dark cloth.

(*see* opposite), (*see* pages 13–14), (*see* page 28)

Horticultural grit

Some gardeners prefer to cover seeds with a layer of horticultural grit instead of compost, as it provides better drainage and allows a small amount of light to reach the seeds. However, it is more expensive and heavier than compost. Vermiculite or perlite are also used sometimes. Like so many practices in gardening, there is no right or wrong way – it's simply a matter of personal preference. Try out different materials and see which you prefer.

HOW TO sow seeds

1 Fill a small pot or seed tray with fresh seed compost and gently firm and level the surface. Scatter the seeds evenly and thinly across the surface. Large seeds can be individually placed (*see* opposite). Avoid letting any of the seeds touch each other, as this will restrict growth.

2 Sieve or sprinkle a thin layer of compost or horticultural grit over the seeds. Generally, small seeds need to be just covered, but larger ones should have a deeper layer over them. Stand the pot in tepid water until the surface of the compost is damp.

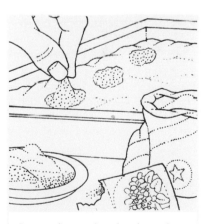

For very fine seed, such as begonias or primulas, mix the seed with fine sand, then sow it in 'pinches' (as shown above) or scatter it evenly over the surface of the compost. Alternatively, put a layer of horticultural grit on the top of the compost and then sow the seed, letting it fall between the tiny particles. Water the pot so that the seed is washed into the compost.

Placing plastic bags over the pots of seed will provide a warm, humid environment that is needed to kick-start germination.

Check seeds daily, dampening the compost if it begins to dry out. At this point it's better to stand the pots and trays in water to wet the compost, since watering the surface may disturb the emerging seedlings.

After germination

When the first seedlings germinate, remove the plastic cover or open the vent in the propagator lid, to give them fresh air. Remove any dead or dying seedlings, and any that are covered in fluffy grey mould, to avoid contaminating neighbouring healthy seedlings.

Where you've sown two seeds to a pot or module, after they germinate remove the weaker of the two seedlings as soon as possible, leaving the other to grow undisturbed. Seedlings sown in trays or two or more to a pot will need to be pricked out (*see* opposite).

The first signs of life: a tiny seedling emerges from the soil, thrusting its way up towards the light.

A tray of seedlings can soon become overcrowded, so you'll need to prick them out (*see* opposite).

Pricking out

One day you'll look at your pots or trays and will see that where there was once bare earth, a forest of seedlings has suddenly emerged. Despite their apparent fragility, it will be time to replant the seedlings, giving them space to grow without being crowded out by their neighbours – a process called 'pricking out'.

Plants are ready to be pricked out when the first true leaves have formed. True leaves look like tiny versions of adult ones, as opposed to the small, rounded 'seed leaves', which emerge first and will soon shrivel. If the seedlings have been grown under heat, harden them off in the greenhouse over a few days once they've germinated before pricking them out (see page 20).

Preparing the container
Most seedlings are best pricked out into individual pots. However, plants that will soon be moved again, such as bedding plants, can be pricked out into trays, provided they're given sufficient space and depth for their root system to expand.

The compost you use for the new pot should be stronger in nutrients than the sowing compost so the plant can grow, but it doesn't need to be particularly strong as the plant is still tiny. If you prefer using a loam-based compost, John Innes No. 1 is ideal (see pages 16–17). Alternatively, use a loamless general-purpose compost. Fill the pot or tray with compost in the same way as you did for seed (see page 26).

Moving the seedlings
Transfer the compost containing the seedlings onto a bench and gently separate the plants, teasing apart the roots. Make a hole in the centre of the new pot of compost, pick up the selected seedling by one of its seed leaves and carefully lower it into the hole, so that it sits at the same depth as it was in its original container. Fill the hole around the roots with the adjacent compost. Put only one seedling per pot, and if using a tray ensure that the seedlings are well spaced apart. Label and water the seedlings and place them in a bright place out of direct sunlight.

Transplanting to the open garden
When you finally come to plant seedlings in the open garden, the procedure is more or less the same as pricking out, except that the plants are grown on until they are much larger, with several sets of leaves. Make sure the soil is cultivated to a fine tilth first, and water well before and after planting.

HOW TO prick out seedlings

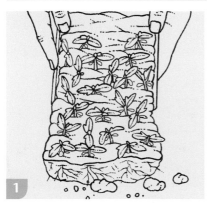

1 When young seedlings have two true leaves, they can be pricked out into individual pots or modules, or spaced wider apart in trays. Water the plants about an hour beforehand, tap the tray and then ease out the compost.

2 Using a dibber or plant label, carefully separate individuals from the group. Hold them by their seed leaves, which have now served their purpose, never by their stems or roots, and ease the roots out of the mass as gently as possible.

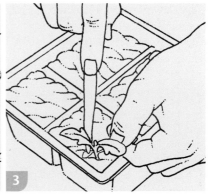

3 Plant the seedlings individually into pre-prepared containers. Gently firm the compost around their roots and water them in well. Protect the seedlings from high temperatures and bright light for a few days until they are established.

Ferns are unlike most other plants in that they propagate themselves in a totally different way, reproducing by spores in a two-stage process – germination, then fertilization – instead of seeds. Many gardeners find it fascinating and propagate ferns just out of interest, not necessarily because they want more plants. Ferns can also be propagated in other ways, namely by rooting bulbils or plantlets and dividing plants (*see* opposite).

Growing from spores

If you look at the underside of a mature fern frond (leaf) you'll see sporangia, which contain the spores (*see* right). Unripe sporangia are usually pale green or pale brown, turning a darker brown as they ripen, which in the case of most temperate ferns generally occurs in mid- to late summer (tropical ferns ripen throughout the year).

When the sporangia are ripe, they swell and split open to release the fine, dust-like spores, which then germinate and develop into 'prothalli', which contain both male and female organs.

The second stage involves the male sperm swimming to a female egg to fertilize it. An embryo develops, later becoming a recognizable fern, which in turn matures and produces spores, continuing the cycle. Moisture is necessary for the sperm to swim to the female, which is why ferns grow in damp places.

When the fronds are laid on paper they drop spores onto the surface, creating an impression of the leaf.

How to propagate from spores

■ When the sporangia on the underside of the fronds are ripe, lay the fronds on a sheet of paper in a warm, draught-free place and the spores will drop onto it. Place the spores in a paper bag, ready for sowing. Ripened spores are best sown fresh, but you can store them in an envelope in the fridge.

■ To make certain that everything is sterile, which is vital when growing ferns, pour boiling water over the empty pot to sterilize it. Fill the pot with compost, then cover it with a piece of kitchen paper and pour boiling water over it. Remove the paper.

■ When the compost has cooled down, sprinkle the spores over the surface, stand the pot in a tray of water and cover with a polythene bag held in place with an elastic band. Place the tray and pot in a warm, bright place but not in direct sunlight.

■ After a few weeks, a green slime appears on the surface of the compost. This signifies that the spores have germinated, but the slime does not contain young ferns, as the spores have not yet been fertilized. Keep the tray topped up with water, as moisture is essential, and leave the polythene on.

■ When small ferns begin to appear on the prothalli, gradually open the

The magnificent fronds of *Asplenium scolopendrium*, with their ripe, rusty-orange sporangia on the underside.

polythene bag and slowly harden off the young plants inside so they acclimatize gradually (*see* page 20).

■ Lift a number of young plants in one lump and transfer them, without breaking up the clump, into another pot filled with fresh fibrous compost (peat substitute). Repeat for all the plants. Once they start growing away, repot ferns singly into pots or discard some of the weaker ones, leaving just one in each of the original pots.

Possible problems

Propagating ferns by spores is enjoyable and intriguing, and is a good method where lots of plants are required, but it can be tricky. Spores may not form in certain conditions, various cultivars may not resemble the parent if propagated from spores and some types are sterile.

Growing from bulbils

A few ferns produce bulbils, some of which develop into tiny plants with roots. They appear either at the frond tips, on the frond's upper surface, or on, under or at the base of the midrib. While there are not many ferns that do this, it is an easy way of increasing those that do. Some of the *Polystichum* ferns, such as *P. setiferum*, and *Asplenium bulbiferum* both produce bulbils.

When the bulbils appear (they look like little scaly lumps), detach the frond from the fern and peg it down onto a tray of potting compost. Water lightly, then place it in a propagator or polythene bag, ensuring the the plastic does not touch the frond. After a short time, roots will appear from the bulbils. Once these are growing strongly, the new plantlets can be detached from the parent plant and potted up.

When there are only a few bulbils near the base of a frond, do not detach the frond but peg it down, still on the plant, into some moist, gritty compost.

Bulbils can develop roots while still on the parent plant. This fresh green plantlet is ready for detaching from the parent frond and potting up.

Some ferns lend themselves to certain methods of propagation.

① *Polypodium vulgare* (common polypody) is one of the easiest ferns to propagate by spores.

② *Asplenium bulbiferum* is best propagated by rooting bulbils.

③ Large clumps of *Dryopteris filix-mas* can be lifted, divided and replanted.

How to propagate common ferns

TYPE OF FERN	PROPAGATION METHODS
Adiantum (Maidenhair fern)	Spores, division
Asplenium (Spleenwort)	Spores, division, bulbils
Athyrium (Lady fern)	Spores, division, bulbils
Blechnum (Hard or water fern)	Spores, division
Dicksonia (Tree fern)	Spores, offsets from trunks
Dryopteris (Buckler fern)	Spores, division (especially cultivars)
Matteuccia (Ostrich fern)	Spores, offsets from runners
Onoclea (Sensitive fern)	Spores, division
Osmunda	Spores, division
Polypodium (Polypody)	Spores, division, bulbils
Polystichum (Shield fern)	Spores, division, bulbils

Division

Division is a good, easy method of producing small quantities of ferns. In some cases where ferns do not produce spores it is the only way. The best time for dividing ferns is in early spring, just before growth starts. It is possible to divide them using two garden forks back to back, avoiding piercing any crowns (*see* page 57). Alternatively, shake or wash the soil from the roots and then divide the crowns, cutting between them with a clean knife where necessary. Each division must have a crown (a growing bud) attached to it. Replant the divisions and throw away any dead material from the centre or edges of the clump.

Sowing direct into the ground

While sowing in pots often gives seedlings a better start in life, it is quite possible – and often preferable – to sow directly into the soil. This is normal practice with most vegetables and also with many annuals and biennials. It is far less labour intensive to sow a couple of rows of vegetables than it is to grow them in a hundred pots and then plant them out. Also, many plants, such as carrots, resent root disturbance and so grow better if they're left undisturbed in the soil rather than transplanted.

Flowers for direct sowing

Calendula officinalis
Centaurea cyanus
Clarkia elegans
Consolida ajacis
Eschscholzia californica
Iberis umbellata
Linaria maroccana
Myosotis
Nemophila
Nigella
Papaver rhoeas
Papaver somniferum
Salvia viridis
Tagetes
Tropaeolum (most)

Preparing the soil

As with growing in pots, the first consideration when sowing seed is the soil, which must be well prepared. Dig it over in autumn, adding well-rotted organic material such as garden compost or farmyard manure; alternatively, you can just spread the organic matter thickly over the surface, and worms and other organisms will work it into the soil before the main growing season.

Leave the soil over winter for the frost and rain to break it down, then fork and rake into a fine tilth in the spring, before sowing. You're aiming for a 5–8cm (2–3in) depth of fine soil, which will allow even the smallest of vegetable seeds to grow through it.

Before sowing, work in some fertilizer and water the area or the rows to be planted, preferably an hour or so before sowing, although there is no need to do this if the soil is moist from recent rain.

If the weather is bad in spring, wait until it improves before sowing. If it is too cold, the seeds won't germinate, and if it's too wet, many seeds will rot before they have a chance to germinate.

Sowing methods

There are two basic methods of sowing seed: broadcasting and in rows. Broadcasting is used primarily for sowing annuals in a border, where seed is scattered randomly

In spring, rake over the soil where you're planning to sow and remove weeds and large stones as you go.

over prepared ground to create a natural, informal effect. If sown in drifts (*see* below), they can produce large areas of colour. Broadcasting is also now used a lot for block sowing of vegetables.

The disadvantage of sowing randomly rather than in rows is that you won't initially be able to identify seedlings from weedlings.

Don't forget

Nearly all commercial seed merchants give recommended sowing depths, distance between rows and thinning distances on the packets. See the directory for details of individual vegetables, pages 88–91.

Nursery beds

Winter vegetables, such as sprouting broccoli, cabbages and leeks, are often raised in nursery beds, where they can be sown quite densely. Once they reach about 15–20cm (6–8in) high, they must be dug up – be careful not to damage the roots – and planted at their recommended spacings in the beds where they are to crop.

Sowing in rows is the traditional way of growing vegetables. The advantage of this method is that it's easy to walk and weed between the rows, air can circulate easily around the plants and the seedlings can be distinguished from the weeds. Biennials, such as wallflowers (*Erysimum*), are also often grown in rows before transplanting out into their beds in autumn for flowering the following year. Many perennials can be grown this way too if you're into mass production, but generally just a few sown in a pot will suffice.

How to sow in rows

Draw out a shallow drill, or groove, in which to sow the seeds. To ensure straight rows, use a garden line (a string held taut between two sticks) as a guide. Pull the corner of a hoe

Mark out each seed row using string tied to two canes and draw the corner of a hoe along the line to make a drill.

along the line, displacing a shallow depression in the soil; alternatively, you can use a bamboo cane or the back of a rake or trowel. The finer the seed, the shallower the drill will need to be. So most vegetable seed, including carrots or radishes, need a drill only 1cm (½in) or so deep, while beans should be 5cm (2in).

HOW TO broadcast sow in drifts

1 Fork over and then rake the soil so that it is level and has a fine surface that the seedlings can easily grow through. Use sand to mark areas to be sown.

2 Within each area, make several shallow depressions, or drills, using the back of a rake or a bamboo cane. Sow the seeds by sprinkling them thinly along the rows.

3 Cover the seeds with a thin layer of soil, water, then protect the whole area with twiggy branches to prevent birds and other animals from disturbing them.

Sprinkle the seed thinly along the drill at spacings recommended on the packet, then mark the row by putting small stakes or sticks at each end. For larger vegetables, such as parsnips, which normally grow at some distance apart, it's best to station sow. This means to sow at intervals, leaving gaps between the 'stations' so that you're not wasting seed or having to thin unnecessarily. In the case of parsnips, you'd need to sow three seeds at each station which would be at 15–20cm (6–8in) intervals along the drill. If more than one seed germinates at each station, the weaker ones are removed.

Having marked the row, rake or push the soil with your fingers over the seed, being careful not to bury them too deeply beneath the surface. Gently tamp down the soil along the row with the back of a rake to firm it. Finally, water the row with a watering can with a fine rose.

Aftercare

Once you've sown your seed and the plants are growing away, they'll need some regular attention to ensure they do well and produce a good crop. With certain vegetables,

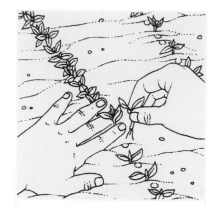

Thinning is important if you want to ensure a good, strong crop. Place your fingers on the soil on either side of the seedling that is to be retained so that it is not disturbed when others are removed.

such as peas and beans, once they start to mature pick regularly, as this tends to promote further cropping.

Protecting plants

Protect new seeds from birds by covering either the whole area in a cage or individual rows with twigs or netting. The only sure way of preventing mice making off with your sown beans and peas is to trap them. Slugs and snails are highly destructive, especially of seedlings

and young plants. Either deter them with copper tape fixed around raised beds, kill them with a bait of your choice, or pick them off every night after dark with the aid of a torch and dispatch them in a pot of salted water.

Watering

Most vegetables like a regular supply of moisture, so water as soon as the ground seems to be dry, but do not turn the vegetable patch into a swamp by overwatering. Generally, there is no need to feed most vegetables if the ground has been well prepared.

Thinning

Seedlings will need thinning to prevent overcrowding and create plenty of space for each remaining plant to develop (*see* above left). Working down each row, pull out weak and damaged seedlings first, then healthy ones too if necessary. Repeat a few times as the plants grow; don't thin to the recommended distances until you're sure each plant you leave is healthy enough to survive. After thinning, water the row.

Weeding

The main problem with broadcast seed is that weeding must be done entirely by hand, whereas it is possible to hoe between rows, although you still have to weed by hand between plants within the rows. Either way, keep a vigilant eye out for weeds and remove them regularly. Weeds compete not only for moisture and nutrients but also for light, and they can be hosts to pests and diseases too.

Sowing in beds under cover

Early vegetables can be grown in beds in greenhouses, polytunnels or cold frames. The method is essentially the same as in the open garden. The only difference is that the soil can become tired, so it is often necessary (especially if growing tomatoes) to replace the soil every year or so. The soil dries out rapidly under cover, so keep the vegetables well watered. Good ventilation is also important for healthy plants.

Easy windowsill projects

Plants are, of course, quite capable of propagating themselves without any of the aids that gardeners have developed, and plenty grow perfectly well without a propagator, greenhouse or potting shed. All you need to get going is a light (but not sunny) windowsill and a few everyday kitchen items, such as a shallow dish or jam jar, kitchen roll, and a pack of seeds or a cutting from a plant you want to reproduce. It's fun to try these really basic forms of propagation in the home, particularly with children, as the results are visible, quick and in some cases edible.

Sprouting seeds on paper

Most of us are introduced to propagation at primary school, and one of the first things we learn is how to grow cress on damp paper. It does seem like a method created for children, but it is a perfectly valid method of propagation – examine the cress in the supermarket and you'll see that it was grown in just the same way.

Many other sprouting seeds can also be grown on paper and are ready to harvest in a matter of days as tiny, nutritious shoots. These include beans (mung beans perhaps being the best known), other podded plants such as peas and lentils, and leafy vegetables, including cabbages (see red cabbage, right), alfalfa and radishes. The shoots are delicious in salads, sandwiches or stir-fry dishes, and are healthy, too.

To grow sprouting seeds, place a sheet of kitchen paper on a shallow dish, such as a saucer or plate, then a second sheet on top of the first. Wet the paper and drain off excess water.

You don't need a garden to propagate plants; a kitchen windowsill will suffice.
① Red cabbage sprouts are ready to harvest after little over a week.
② Many house plants (here, *Chlorophytum* and *Iresine*) root easily in a glass of water.
③ Mint cuttings ready for potting up.

Plants that root easily in water

Begonia	Impatiens
Coleus	Mentha
Cyperus	Penstemon
Fuchsia	Plectranthus
Hedera	Rosmarinus

Scatter seed thickly over the paper and place the dish on a warm, bright windowsill, preferably not in direct sunlight. Keep the paper moist but not saturated. After a few days, the seed begins to germinate, and once the shoots are about 2–3cm (1in) high (usually after about five to ten days), they're ready to harvest using a pair of scissors. Rinse the shoots and use them as soon as possible.

Jam-jar cuttings

Cuttings from many plants, particularly house plants, can be induced to produce roots simply by placing them in water. Many soft-stemmed perennials, herbs, and even a number of woody house plants, can also be treated in this way.

All you need is a glass jar half-filled with water and a tip cutting from a young shoot (see pages 37 and 41). Pop the cutting into the water so that roughly the bottom third is covered by it and place the jar on a bright but not sunny windowsill. You may need to use wire netting to keep the cutting in place. Within a few weeks in some cases, little buds will appear at the base of the cutting, and these will gradually elongate into roots. When healthy roots have developed, pot up the plants into individual pots of compost in the usual way (see page 42).

Growing from cuttings

Many perennial and shrubby plants can be grown easily from cuttings, enabling the gardener to create exact copies of the parent plant. It is particularly useful for replicating rare plants and for propagating those that don't produce viable seed or whose seed doesn't come 'true' (that is, the seedlings differ from the parent). Also, you get bigger plants more quickly than if you're sowing seed. Raising plants from cuttings is very straightforward – anyone can do it, and the equipment required is minimal, so just give it a go.

Types of cutting

A cutting is part of a plant that has been snipped off and inserted into a pot of compost; after a while, roots develop and a new plant is formed. Not all plants are easy to root in this way, but a surprising number are, particularly herbaceous perennials. There are several types of cutting taken from different parts of the plant. Most are cut from the shoots, and generally they're treated in the same way with just minor variations (*see* pages 37–47). However, some cuttings are taken from a plant's leaves (*see* pages 48–9) or roots (*see* pages 50–1).

Tip cuttings

This is the commonest group of cuttings, and many (but not all) perennials, as well as some woody plants, can be propagated in this way. Each cutting consists of the top portion, or tip, of a shoot.

The length of the cutting varies according to the type of plant, but it should consist of at least two leaf

Shoot cuttings

Most cuttings are taken from a plant's shoots, or stems. Depending on the type of plant, you can take cuttings from the tip, a section of the stem or base of a shoot, or from a sideshoot (as in leaf-bud and heel cuttings). Cuttings from woody plants have several variants depending on the time of year you take the cuttings (*see* pages 44–7).

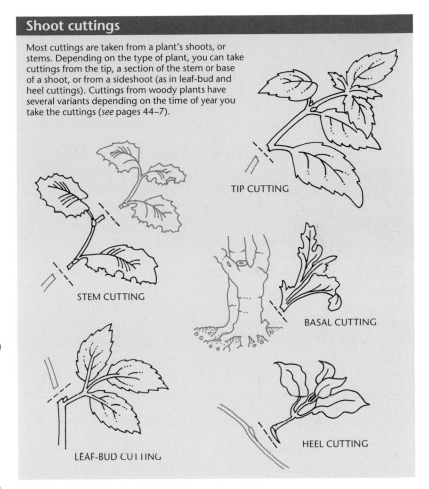

TIP CUTTING

STEM CUTTING

BASAL CUTTING

LEAF-BUD CUTTING

HEEL CUTTING

nodes (where the leaves join the stem), and a bud at the top. In most cases, the cutting has more than two nodes, especially in short-stemmed plants where the nodes are very close together, such as in alpine plants. For details on how to take a tip cutting, *see* page 41.

Stem cuttings

The stems of some plants, particularly perennials, root very easily and it's possible to use sections of stem, not just the tip. The benefit of this method is you can get several cuttings from one stem, so less is wasted. Select a plant with two or more leaf nodes. Generally, the stem is cut immediately above and below a node, although occasionally internodal cuttings are more appropriate (*see* box, page 38).

Don't forget

Stems that contain flowers or flower buds are not suitable as cutting material, so choose non-flowering shoots if possible. However, in some cases, such as pelargoniums or busy lizzies (*Impatiens*), you may not have an option, so remove flowers and buds from cuttings.

When choosing a shoot for cutting (here, *Ribes*), select a healthy, non-flowering stem. Regular pruning of woody plants will stimulate vigorous new growth.

Taking stem cuttings

Normally, stem cuttings are taken with the base cut immediately below and the top cut immediately above a node (the place where the leaf joins the stem); these are known as 'nodal cuttings'. In most cases, disease is less likely to be introduced to the stem this way and the plant is more likely to produce roots. However, a few plants, such as diascias, clematis and more mature woody plants, root better if the bottom cut is made equidistant between two nodes (the top cut is still made immediately above a node); this is known as 'internodal'. Nodal and internodal cuttings are prepared in the same way.

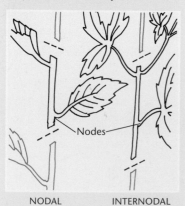

NODAL   INTERNODAL

Penstemons propagate easily by stem cuttings, and if you're new to gardening it's worth experimenting with these first. Some woody plants also propagate in this way.

Basal cuttings

Not all perennials can root from cuttings from mature stems, so in such cases you'll need to use the young growth as it first emerges at the base of the plant, usually in spring. Good examples of plants that are propagated this way are violas and some asters. Take the

Pre-rooted cuttings

Sometimes when removing basal cuttings the shoot comes away lower than expected and contains some roots. These can be potted up as ready-rooted cuttings. In a sense, this is really a form of division (see pages 56–9), but it often happens when you're taking cuttings and is quite a valid way of taking them. Plants that tend to do this include some asters, *Anaphalis, Mimulus, Rudbeckia* and *Veronica*.

shoot off as close as possible to the base and then treat it as a tip cutting (*see* page 41).

Although these types of cuttings are usually taken early in the year, it is possible to stimulate new basal growth at other times by shearing over the whole or part of the plant close to the ground so that new growth appears.

Cuttings from sideshoots

In the case of some woody plants, cuttings are best taken from the sideshoots instead of the main stems. The two main ways of propagating plants from sideshoots are by leaf-bud cuttings, which are similar to stem cuttings but shorter and with only one bud, and heel cuttings, in which a sideshoot is gently peeled from the parent plant (*see* pages 37 and 47).

Leaf and root cuttings

Some plants are propagated by taking cuttings from leaves or roots rather than the shoots. Many house plants propagate easily from leaf cuttings, and root cuttings are in some cases the only way of increasing certain plants that cannot be propagated by any other vegetative method. Also, root cuttings can reduce the chance of particular diseases taking hold in young plants. For more details on leaf cuttings, *see* pages 48–9, and for root cuttings, *see* pages 50–1.

Don't forget

To prevent disease from entering the plant, ensure that you make clean cuts rather than a ragged cut or tear and use clean cutting implements (*see* box, page 19).

Shoot cuttings from perennials

Herbaceous perennials, which die down in winter and produce fresh growth each year, are generally quite easy to propagate from cuttings and are good for beginners. The basic techniques described on these pages apply to most types of shoot cutting and are easy to master. For cuttings taken from leaves or roots, *see* pages 48–51. Cuttings of most perennials can be taken at virtually any time during the growing season, although some are best taken later in the year, after flowering. For details of individual plants, *see* the directory (pages 66–91).

The scented *Pelargonium graveolens* is propagated from tip or stem cuttings taken between spring and autumn.

Taking the cutting

Try to take cuttings in the early morning, when it's cooler and when stems are full of sap, rather than in the middle of a hot day, when the plant is flagging in the heat. It's essential that the cuttings don't dry out, so ideally take the cuttings just before you use them. This may not always be possible, as one of the great joys of gardening is to receive cuttings when visiting friends' gardens and it may be a while before you get back to your potting shed. The softer the wood, the more quickly the cuttings will wilt.

Select a healthy-looking plant, and where possible take the younger, more vigorous, non-flowering shoots from the edge of a clump. The amount of cutting material you take depends on the plant, and the length of the cutting will vary according to the type of plant you're dealing with: alpines are often only a couple of centimetres or so long, while tall herbaceous plants may be

several times that. If you're taking a tip cutting (*see* page 41), you need to take only the top 10cm (4in) or so, providing there are at least two leaf nodes (where the leaf joins the stem). If this will disfigure the plant, take the whole shoot right back to the next junction or to the base,

The pretty, short-lived perennial flax *Linum narbonense* can be increased by cuttings in spring, while the bulbous *Allium cristophii* is propagated from offsets in autumn (*see* pages 60–1).

Delphiniums develop hollow stems, which are difficult to root and can rot in compost. For this reason, it's better to take basal cuttings from fresh young growth.

Perennials that propagate easily from cuttings

TIP CUTTINGS
Argyranthemum
Dianthus
Erysimum
Gypsophila
Lobelia
Osteospermum
Pelargonium
Penstemon
Phygelius
Salvia
Solenostemon

STEM CUTTINGS
Diascia
Lobelia
Oenothera (some)
Pelargonium
Penstemon
Saponaria

BASAL CUTTINGS
Artemisia
Aster (some)
Chrysanthemum
Delphinium
Lupinus
Stachys
Viola

cutting just above a bud or sideshoot so that it can grow away again. For taking stem cuttings, *see* pages 37–8, and for basal cuttings, *see* page 38.

As soon as you've taken the cutting, pop it into a polythene bag, seal it and put it in a cool, shady place (not on the back seat of the car in the sun!) until you're ready to prepare it.

Penstemons (here, *P.* 'Maurice Gibbs') are easy to propagate by either tip cuttings or stem cuttings in spring.

Preparing cuttings

When you're back in the potting shed, or wherever you do your potting, take the cuttings one by one out of the bag.

If you're taking a tip or basal cutting, remove all the leaves on the stem except for the top two and the

Don't forget

Wallflowers (*Erysimum*) and sweet williams (*Dianthus barbatus*) are usually grown as biennials, so tend to be dug up and discarded after flowering in their second year. However, if you take cuttings of your favourites you can enjoy them for several more years.

bud above it. For stem cuttings, remove the lower leaves and perhaps one or two more on leafy stems so there is enough bare stem to insert into the growing medium. Since a cutting has no roots, it draws up only a limited amount of water through its stem and so has difficulty in supporting a large number of leaves. Cut them off neatly using a sharp knife, scalpel or pair of fine-pointed scissors. If you want to shorten the cutting, cut cleanly just below a leaf node.

If the remaining leaves are large, it's often a good idea to cut these in half so that there is not such a large surface area through which to lose moisture. Some penstemons, for example, benefit from this.

Cut the stem just below a node (leaf joint), so that the final length of the cutting is about 5–8cm (2–3in).

Silver-leaved plants

Plants with grey or silvery foliage, such as pinks (*Dianthus*), can be susceptible to too much atmospheric moisture and do not like to be totally enclosed. If you find silver- or grey-leaved plants rotting off, try leaving the vents or lid on the propagator slightly open so that air can circulate. Be careful, though, that the compost does not dry out.

HOW TO take tip cuttings

Remove strong, healthy, non-flowering shoot-tips from the plant that you wish to propagate. The cuttings should be up to about 10cm (4in) long.

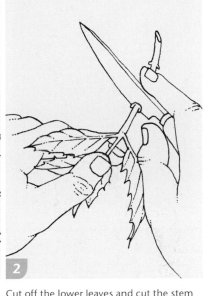

Cut off the lower leaves and cut the stem cleanly, with a sharp knife, just below a node, to leave a neat cutting about 5–8cm (2–3in) long.

Insert cuttings around the edge of a pot of compost, spaced out so that they are not touching each other. If you like, dip the cut ends of the cuttings in hormone rooting powder or gel first.

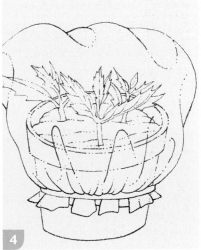

Water the pot and cover with a plastic bag to keep humidity high – or put the pot in a propagator. Check regularly and pot on when new growth indicates that the cuttings have rooted.

When a cutting has developed a good root system, it is ready to be transferred to another, larger pot.

Promoting rooting

Fill a pot or seed tray with cutting compost, tap it on the bench to settle the compost and then gently firm it down. Make a hole in the compost with a small dibber or pencil, close to but not actually touching the edge of the pot, and insert the cutting to about half its length. Firm the compost gently round the cutting and then do the same for the remaining cuttings, placing them a sufficient distance apart that the leaves don't touch. For small cuttings, you can get about six around the inside of a 9cm (3½in) pot; about three if they have large leaves.

Once the cuttings are all inserted round the pot, water the compost lightly. Place the pot into a propagator (see pages 13–14) or cover it with a polythene bag, making sure that neither the side of the propagator nor the bag touches the cuttings. Place in a warm but not hot position in plenty of light, but avoid direct sunlight.

Keep an eye on the cuttings. Do not allow them to dry out, but at the same time do not allow condensation on the inside of the propagator or polythene bag to drip onto the foliage. A good practice is to take the lid off the propagator daily and dry the inside of it. Similarly, remove the plastic bag and turn it inside out so the condensation is now on the outside and evaporates.

Potting up cuttings

It's impossible to say exactly how long it takes for cuttings to root, as timings can vary considerably, but it's usually obvious when the cuttings begin to grow away. Often, you'll see roots coming out of the holes at the base of the pot, and this is a sure sign that it's time to transfer the cuttings into their own, individual pots.

If you're unsure, tap the pot on the bench and turn it upside down, resting the compost on your hand with your fingers between the cuttings. The pot will easily slide off and you can see what roots have formed. If none or only small ones have appeared, slide the pot back on, turn it up the right way and tap it on the bench again to settle the compost; if this is done carefully, the cuttings should remain intact.

When potting up, use a richer potting compost (see pages 16–17) and increase the size of pots gradually as the plants get larger ('potting on'). Before taking plants grown under cover outdoors, harden them off so they can get used to the lower temperatures (see page 20).

A cold frame is ideal for hardening off plants that have been grown under cover, enabling them to acclimatize gradually to cooler outdoor temperatures.

Succulents

Succulents, including cacti, are a special category of plants. To most amateur gardeners, they are generally considered to be house plants, although some are grown in the open garden. Cacti are generally propagated only by specialist growers and are beyond the scope of this book. However, most common succulents are relatively easy to propagate in several ways.

Sowing seed

Succulents produce seed that can be sown in pots or trays in the same way as other plants (*see* pages 26–8). It's usually best to sow seed fresh, as soon as you harvest it. In the case of bought seed, sow it as soon as possible after purchase (usually in spring).

Taking cuttings

You can take shoot cuttings from the tips and stems of many succulents as you would for herbaceous perennials (*see* pages 39–40). The best time to do this is in spring, but cuttings from winter-flowering succulents are best taken in autumn. One major difference between succulents and other cuttings is that there is no need to put them in polythene bags to keep them fresh once you've taken the cutting. Indeed, with many you need to leave them uncovered in a warm, dry, airy place for the cut to callus over, which may take several days or even weeks.

Most succulents can also be increased by leaf cuttings. This simple process involves removing a leaf and placing it into a pot or tray of compost until roots form (*see* pages 48–9).

Easy to propagate

Agave	Kalanchoe
Crassula	Pachyphytum
Echeveria	Rhodiola
Euphorbia	Sedum
Haworthia	Sempervivum

When taking cuttings of succulents, it's important to use a suitable growing medium – the compost needs to be free-draining and low in nutrients; a mixture of equal amounts of John Innes No. 1 compost (*see* pages 16–17) and sharp sand is ideal. Bury the callused part of the cutting and lightly dampen the soil, but make sure you don't soak it. Place the pot or tray in a bright but not sun-scorched spot. Do not let it dry out, but on the other hand do little more than dampen it.

Once the cuttings have roots, pot them up into a free-draining compost; you could use a proprietary compost for succulents, or multipurpose compost with horticultural grit added (*see* box, page 27). Harden off plants grown under cover over a few days or several weeks to get them used to colder temperatures (*see* page 20).

Dividing plants

Many of the larger, clump-forming succulents, for instance *Sedum spectabile*, can be divided in the same way as clump-forming perennials (*see* pages 56–8), usually in spring.

A great number of succulents, particularly rosette-forming plants such as *Sempervivum*, produce 'offsets' (new young plants) around the parent plant. These are easily detached in spring, usually by gently pulling them off the parent (*see* right), ensuring you retain a bit of the stem. Replant the offsets in pots filled with free-draining compost,

Succulents can be propagated in a number of ways.

① *Kalanchoe blossfeldiana* cultivars (here, 'Catalana') are most easily propagated from leaf cuttings.

② Sempervivums produce offsets (rosettes) that can be detached from the parent and replanted elsewhere.

setting the base just below the surface of the compost. If the plant doesn't have roots, don't worry, as these will soon develop.

To detach the rosettes of offset-forming plants (here, *Echeveria*), pull gently or use a clean, sharp knife to sever the stem.

Shoot cuttings from woody plants

Since plants with woody stems, such as trees, shrubs and many climbers, cannot usually be divided, cuttings are an invaluable propagation method. Many root relatively easily, but there are some that are difficult and very slow. Generally, more patience is required with woody cuttings than with perennials. Most cuttings from woody plants are tip cuttings, but some plants also root from cuttings taken from the stem (*see* pages 37–8).

Types of cutting

Cuttings of woody plants are defined in many ways and can be confusing to the beginner. Try not to get bogged down with all the terms – nothing beats just getting on with it and learning by experience – but it may increase your chances of success if you're familiar with the various stages of growth so you know when to take cuttings for best chances of success.

Woody cuttings are often categorized by the ripeness of the wood, depending on the season, so we find there are softwood, greenwood, semi-ripe and hardwood cuttings. Choosing the method to suit the plant you want to propagate is very important for success, although some can be propagated in various ways. For details on particular plants, *see* box, opposite, and the directory, pages 66–91.

Softwood

This is wood taken from plants early in the season, soon after the shoots have burst into leaf – usually in spring, but it can be later depending on the plant. The stems tend to be quite soft, fleshy and pliable, full of vigour and most likely to develop roots. This method is suitable for most deciduous shrubs and various, primarily deciduous trees.

Greenwood

By early and midsummer, the wood has hardened slightly yet the stems are still quite pliable. The roots form less easily than from softwood cuttings, but greenwood cuttings need less care and are more likely to survive. They are suitable for most deciduous and some evergreen plants. If you miss the softwood season, greenwood cuttings usually root just as well.

Semi-ripe

By mid- to late summer and early autumn, the wood has hardened considerably and growth has started to slow. Roots take much longer to establish than from softwood or greenwood, but the cuttings are much more resilient. Semi-ripe cuttings are successful with a wide range of shrubs and trees, both deciduous and evergreen.

Hardwood

By early winter, the wood is usually fully ripe, the plant is dormant and the cuttings will survive without attention, although they may take several months to develop any roots. This method is suitable for many deciduous shrubs and trees.

Cuttings of hebes (here, *H.* 'Watson's Pink') are best taken in late summer or early autumn, when the current year's growth has just started to turn woody (semi-ripe).

Taking softwood, greenwood and semi-ripe cuttings

For softwood, greenwood and semi-ripe cuttings, the procedure is very similar to that of tip cuttings of herbaceous plants (see pages 39–42), except it takes a little longer as you're using thicker material.

It is particularly important that softwood cuttings are not allowed to dry out, and you need to keep

When selecting softwood cuttings (here, *Fuchsia*), remove the stem immediately above a leaf node, about 10–12cm (4–5in) from the tip.

Insert semi-ripe cuttings (here, *Ribes*) into trays or pots of moist, well-drained compost so about one third of the stem sits below the surface.

humidity high until roots form, so put them into a polythene bag as soon as you cut them and, again, straight into a closed propagator as soon as you've prepared them. If you don't have a propagator, a plastic bag covering the pot will be fine.

Greenwood and semi-ripe cuttings are a bit tougher than the softwood type, but they still mustn't dry out. If the tip of the shoot is at all soft, it's a good idea to remove it just above a node (where a leaf or pair of leaves joins on to the main stem).

Taking hardwood cuttings

Hardwood cuttings require a different technique. They are taken after leaf fall and before new growth starts in spring, from late autumn to midwinter, and can be put outdoors, either in a large pot or straight into the ground (see page 46).

The length isn't critical, but they're usually about 15–23cm (6–9in) long, with a cut above and below a bud at each end. When

Easily propagated plants

SOFTWOOD CUTTINGS

Abutilon
Betula
Deutzia
Fuchsia
Hydrangea
Lonicera
Philadelphus
Prunus

GREENWOOD CUTTINGS

Ceanothus
Forsythia
Philadelphus
Ribes
Rubus

SEMI-RIPE CUTTINGS

Aucuba
Berberis
Cotoneaster
Ilex
Laurus
Mahonia
Prunus lusitanica

HARDWOOD CUTTINGS

Cornus
Elaeagnus
Forsythia
Prunus laurocerasus
Salix
Tamarix

Hormone rooting preparations

Traditionally, cuttings are dipped in a rooting hormone, which may be in liquid or powder form, before being inserted into the soil. Gardeners' opinions on the value of this vary, but generally most find some plants, particularly woody plants, root better if a hormone preparation is used. In the case of easy-to-root cuttings it appears to make little difference. One of the main benefits of these preparations is that the powder or liquid usually contains a fungicide that helps to keep diseases at bay.

If you decide to use a rooting hormone, dip only the base of the cutting into the compound and tap off the surplus. Hormone rooting preparations tend to deteriorate with age, so replace annually.

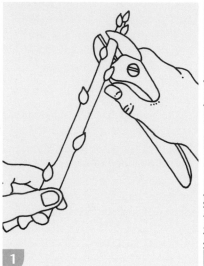

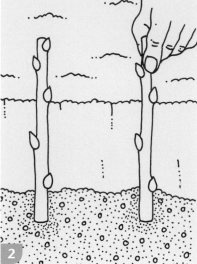

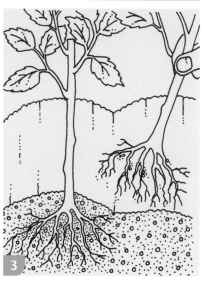

1 Remove a healthy stem from the current year's growth, making a straight cut just below a node. Cut off any sideshoots, then trim off the top, making a sloping cut just above a bud. The cutting should be about 15–23cm (6–9in) long. Dip the base in hormone rooting preparation, if using.

2 Dig a small trench in the garden and refill it with a mixture of sharp sand and soil; firm the soil mix. Make a continuous slit in it with a spade. Insert the cuttings at least 5cm (2in) apart and so that only the top third is visible. Backfill, firm the soil, label the cuttings and water them in.

3 Leave the cuttings until they come into leaf and have developed a good root system, which will not be until at least the spring. Water during the growing season and weed regularly, then dig up the plants in autumn and either replant them in the open garden or pot them up into individual pots.

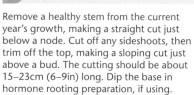

you've prepared the cutting, make a slit trench in a sheltered place in the garden and insert the cuttings into the trench as shown above. Water and leave the cuttings until the leaves appear and the root system is established (usually spring at the earliest), then lift the new plants in autumn to make sure that the roots have developed and replant them.

If you're putting hardwood cuttings into a pot, fill it with free-draining cutting compost and make a small slit trench in the compost before inserting the cuttings. Place the pot in a cold frame or stand it in a well-lit, frost-free, sheltered spot outside over winter.

Cuttings from sideshoots

Heel cuttings and leaf-bud cuttings are two quite different methods of taking cuttings from sideshoots rather than the main stems of woody plants.

Evergreen cuttings

Generally, the cuttings of evergreen plants are taken in late summer or autumn, when the wood has hardened a little. Take heel cuttings (*see* opposite) and use a hormone rooting preparation (*see* box, page 45) if you wish, then proceed as for other cuttings. If the leaves are large, reduce them by half with a clean cut across the leaf. For larger quantities (say, of a hedging plant), rather than using a pot put them directly into the soil of a propagator. Conifer cuttings are taken in the same way, although not all such plants are easy to propagate from cuttings.

Heel cuttings

Some woody cuttings are taken with a 'heel' (*see* opposite). This heel has a greater propensity to produce roots than the cutting by itself. Evergreens, particularly those with hollow or pithy stems, are best taken with heels, as are plants that are old or in less than peak condition, as they tend to root more easily this way. Heel cuttings are suitable for most types of conifer.

Leaf-bud cuttings

Leaf-bud cuttings are made in the same way as stem cuttings and are taken from any type of wood; they are most commonly used for propagating camellias and mahonias. The main difference is that they are shorter than stem cuttings, and make more economical use of material from the parent plant. Each piece of stem must contain a leaf and a leaf-bud, which will become the stem of the new plant (*see* below).

Easily propagated from sideshoots

HEEL CUTTINGS
Berberis
Ceanothus
Erica
Hypericum
Pieris
Sambucus

LEAF-BUD CUTTINGS
Camellia
Clematis
Hedera
Lonicera
Mahonia

HOW TO take heel cuttings

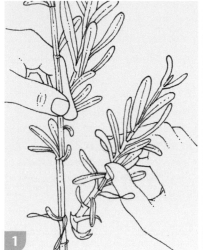

1 Carefully peel a sideshoot downwards, away from the main stem, so that part of the old wood of the stem (the heel) comes away with the cutting. Remove the lower leaves from the bottom half to two thirds of the stem and pinch out the shoot tip. Trim the heel and dip the base in hormone rooting preparation, if required.

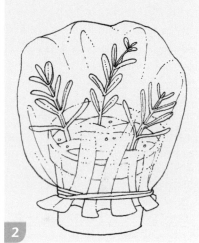

2 Insert the cuttings around the edge of a pot filled with cutting compost. Water the pot well and put it in a sheltered spot in the garden or in a cold frame. Smaller cuttings may root more easily if covered with a plastic bag, but don't let them dry out. When the cuttings have rooted, plant them out or pot them up individually.

HOW TO take leaf-bud cuttings

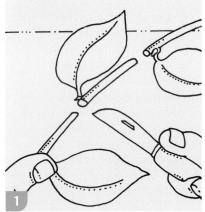

1 Make a clean cut immediately above a leaf and another cut about 3–4cm (1¼–1¾in) below it. Each cutting needs to have a leaf-bud, which lies in the axil (the angle where the leaf-stalk joins the stem).

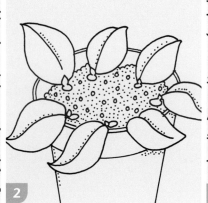

2 If the leaves are large, cut them in half. Insert the cuttings into cutting compost so the stem is below the surface but the leaf and leaf-bud are lying on top, then treat the cuttings as for heel cuttings (*see* above).

3 The following spring, a fresh new shoot will emerge from the leaf-bud and new roots will form. When the roots have properly developed, the young plants are ready to plant out or pot up.

Leaf cuttings

There are a few plants that can be increased from leaf cuttings. Of these, a few are herbaceous plants, but the majority are what in temperate climates are thought of as house plants. The leaves of suitable plants are removed from the parent plant in spring or summer and are either used whole or cut into pieces to get identical plants. For all the methods described, fill a pot or tray with cutting compost and insert the cuttings as described. Once they have rooted well, pot them up individually.

To prepare cut-leaf cuttings, cut the leaf into sections, about 4cm (1½in) apart, slicing across the main vein.

Leaves with stalks

For plants that have leaves on stalks, such as African violets (*Saintpaulia*) and smooth-leaved begonias (not *Begonia rex*), this is a very easy technique. You simply remove a healthy, mature leaf from the parent plant, including its leaf-stalk, and insert it into cutting compost as shown below. A few months later, a new plantlet will emerge from the base of the stalk.

Leaves without stalks

Some leaves that don't have stalks are stimulated to grow new plants from their base once they have been removed from the parent plant. The commonest example of plants that are propagated in this way are those perennials with succulent leaves, for instance *Sedum aizoon, S. telephium and S. spectabile*, known as ice plants. Although some sedums are grown as house plants, the majority are planted outdoors in the garden, particularly the taller ones.

Remove the leaves from the plant and keep them in a cool place. After a few days, once they have callused over, push their bases into a tray of compost, inserting them upright or at an angle, making sure they don't touch each other, then treat as for leaves with stalks (*see* step 2, left).

Cut-leaf cuttings

Some plants with long foliage, such as Cape primroses (*Streptocarpus*) and mother-in-law's tongue (*Sansevieria*), can be easily propagated by cutting the leaf into sections, as shown above.

After preparing the leaves, make shallow slits in the compost and insert the cut sections of leaf, placing them upright and the right

HOW TO take leaf cuttings

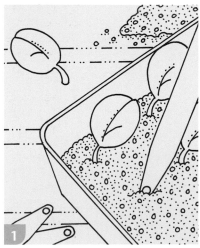

1

Using a sharp knife, cut a mature leaf from a plant, including 4cm (1½in) of leaf-stalk. Make an angled hole in the compost using a dibber or pencil, insert the leaf-stalks and firm in. The leaves should be lying back at an angle.

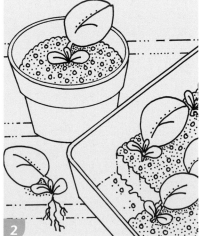

2

Put the cuttings in a warm, humid, light place, out of direct sun, ideally in a heated propagator. Alternatively, cover in a plastic bag. A new plantlet will grow from the base of the stalk. When the young plants are big enough to handle, pot them up.

Suitable for leaf cuttings

Begonia	Saintpaulia
Crassula	Sansevieria
Echeveria	Sedum
Kalanchoe	Streptocarpus

HOW TO take cuttings by leaf slashing

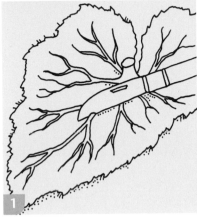

1 Place the leaf upside down on a board, and, using a clean, sharp scalpel, make about four or five cuts across the leaf veins on the underside of the leaf.

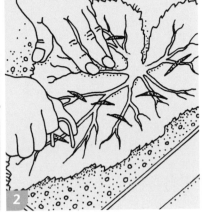

2 Turn the leaf over, and pin it down with bent wire or paper clips bent open to make U-shaped pins. The cut veins must make contact with the compost.

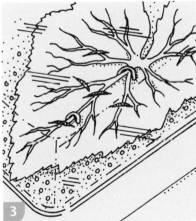

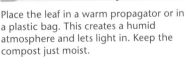

3 Place the leaf in a warm propagator or in a plastic bag. This creates a humid atmosphere and lets light in. Keep the compost just moist.

4 In approximately a couple of months' time, tiny plants will appear from each slash in the leaf. When they are large enough to handle, pot them up.

way up. The bottom 1cm (½in) of leaf section should be buried and the rest left protruding. Keep in a warm propagator until the cuttings have rooted (they tend to develop where the cut is), then pot them up.

Leaf slashing

A few plants, including *Begonia rex*, can be propagated from a whole leaf, but instead of inserting it into compost as you do for other leaf cuttings, you cut slits in it and simply lay it on the surface of the compost, held down with pins so it can make contact with the soil (*see* left). In time, tiny plants will appear where the cuts were made.

Leaf-square cuttings

Begonia rex responds reasonably well to the leaf-square cutting technique (*see* below). Cut the underside of the leaf evenly into long strips, then into 2cm (¾in) squares; each square must have a main vein running through it. Turn the squares over and lay them on the compost, veins downward, then continue as for leaf slashing (*see* left).

For leaf-square cuttings, cut the leaf underside into squares, turn them over and lay them on compost.

Secret of success

The key to success with leaf cuttings is to prevent wilting (caused by dehydration) and fungal infection. To prevent dehydration, check often to see if cuttings need watering and keep their compost just moist all the time. Cover all but hairy, felty or succulent cuttings with a lid to keep them humid.

However, don't create a damp fug, or this will encourage rotting. Also, don't overwater. Instead, place the tray or pot into another tray containing water and let the compost become wet from beneath. Remove leaves that fall off or start to die, and ventilate the cuttings, particularly on hot days.

Root cuttings

Anyone who has left a piece of dandelion root in the soil when weeding will know how easy it is to produce a new plant from such a fragment. Root cuttings are basically just sections of root in the same way as shoot cuttings are sections of stem. However, unlike shoot cuttings, which are just snipped from the growing plant, with root cuttings you have to dig up the parent plant first. The idea of taking root cuttings can seem a bit daunting to novice propagators, but it's actually a very simple process.

The bright scarlet blooms of the perennial oriental poppies (*Papaver orientale*) make a spectacular display from late spring to midsummer. They reproduce naturally from broken roots left in the soil, so lend themselves perfectly to root cuttings.

Dig up the plant that you want to propagate. Chop off one or two of the thick, young roots, then replant the parent plant.

Why take root cuttings?

Generally, root cuttings are taken from tap-rooted plants that cannot be propagated any other vegetative way. For example, the oriental poppy (*Papaver orientale*) cannot be easily divided, nor can conventional cuttings be taken. It can be grown from seed, but you won't get an identical plant to the original. The only way you can do this in this instance is by root cuttings.

There is quite a different reason for propagating *Phlox* using root cuttings. You can increase it from stem cuttings or division, but phlox suffers from a disease caused by eel worms and this is transmitted to the young plants if you use these methods. However, this does not happen when using root cuttings, so you can produce new, disease-free plants.

Taking root cuttings

The best time to take root cuttings is when the plant is dormant. For the majority of plants, this means the winter months. Choose a day in

Plants suitable for root cuttings	
Acanthus	Eryngium
Anchusa	Papaver
Anemone	Phlox
Crambe	Pulsatilla
Echinops	Verbascum

take root cuttings

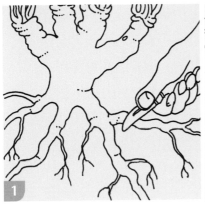

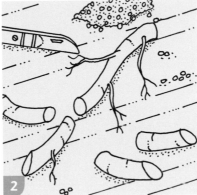

1 Dig up the parent plant when dormant and shake off the soil from the roots. Using a sharp knife, remove one or two youngish but sturdy roots, making a clean cut near the crown of the plant. Discard the thin tip of the root and remove any fibrous sideshoots. Replant the plant once you have taken the cuttings you require.

2 Divide the roots into smaller sections, about 5–10cm (2–4in) long. Cut at right angles across the root at the crown end (this will be the top of the cutting), then lower down make a 45° cut (to indicate the bottom of the cutting). For the next cutting, repeat the procedure, first removing the angled cut created by the previous cutting.

3 Fill a pot or tray with cutting compost. Make a hole in the compost and insert a cutting, angled end first, until the top is level with the surface. Cover the soil and cutting with a thin layer of horticultural grit, water and put in a warm propagator or on the bench in a greenhouse. In spring, when the cuttings have produced roots and leaves, pot them up.

early winter, when the ground isn't frozen or very wet. Plants can be dug up when the ground is wet, but planting isn't a good idea if the soil is like mud, and tramping around on sodden beds will compact the soil.

First, you need to dig up the parent plant. It is possible in a loose, friable soil to excavate down beside a plant and just remove a couple of roots without disturbing it, but generally it's easier to take up the plant completely. If the soil is loose, it can be shaken from the roots, exposing them, but with heavier

soils it may be necessary to wash the soil off with water.

Take cuttings as shown above, and once you've taken what you require, replant the original plant as soon as you can. When preparing the cuttings, make sure you use straight and angled cuts to indicate the top and base of the cuttings respectively. If you make both cuts straight across the plant, you'll find it surprisingly easy to forget which end is top and which is bottom and may insert them upside down in the compost. Some gardeners prefer to plant the cuttings horizontally in the pot, but the general practice is to plant them vertically.

The following spring, when the cuttings have produced roots and leaves, they can be potted up in the usual way.

Don't forget

Remember to label the cuttings as you take them and the pots as you fill them. One root cutting can look very much like the next, and although you may think you'll remember which is which, a moment's distraction can cause all kinds of confusion.

The fresh new growth of *Crambe cordifolia* sprouting from a root cutting taken the previous year.

Layering, division and grafting

As well as sowing seed and taking cuttings, there are other methods of increasing plants that are valuable for gardeners to know about and experiment with. Layering and division are two such, and both are common and very easy methods of vegetative reproduction. Some plants, particularly bulbs, naturally produce new plants ('offsets') around the base of the parent, so propagate almost entirely by themselves. Grafting is a more specialist technique; although it's harder to master, it can be fun and instructive, particularly if you become serious about propagating trees, shrubs and roses.

Layering

Layering takes advantage of the way that many plants (especially woody ones) propagate naturally and simply gives them a helping hand. It is a very easy process that at its most basic requires no tools, no compost and no propagator, although a little help from the gardener will ensure greater success. A wide range of shrubs and climbers can be propagated this way.

When a branch bends over and touches the soil, it can naturally take root and create a new plant at the point of contact. Some plants never become severed from the parent, while in others the connection rots away, leaving a completely separate plant. Although this is a natural process, if you want to propagate particular plants and be assured of success you need to carry out a few simple steps to encourage rooting.

Encouraging layering

A surprising number of plants will layer successfully – if a shrub or climber has strong, whippy shoots

Clematis (here, 'Jenny'), as well as a whole host of other climbers and shrubs with long, flexible shoots, is easily propagated by layering.

Easy to layer

Akebia	Kolkwitzia
Aucuba	Laurus
Campsis	Magnolia
Chaenomeles	Parthenocissus
Clematis	Rosa (ramblers, ground-cover roses and some shrub roses)
Cornus	
Corylopsis	Skimmia
Cotoneaster	Syringa
Hedera	Trachelospermum
Jasminum	

that you can bring down to ground level without any danger of them breaking, it's certainly worth trying. Some plants layer very quickly (*see* box, left), while others can take a long time, even several years.

The great thing about layering is that you can do it as and when the opportunity arises rather than

Don't forget

Young, pliable stems make the best layering material. You can encourage vigorous new growth by pruning the adult plant.

deliberately setting out to do it. For example, when weeding a bed you may suddenly spot a branch that would make an ideal layer and so you can simply do it there and then. However, in the case of most plants, layering in spring or autumn probably gives best results.

There are several different layering techniques. Simple layering is the most common method, but there are also variations that are more suitable for particular plants (*see* pages 54–5).

Simple layering

Choose a healthy, low-growing, whippy stem for layering. If necessary, first prepare the soil where the cutting is to be buried, about 20–30cm (8–12in) from the tip of the shoot. If you have a good loam, simply dig over the area. If the soil is poor, remove the topsoil and refill it with compost with added horticultural grit; a moderate soil can be improved by adding grit and some fibrous material.

The key to successful layering is to restrict the supply of food to the tip of the shoot, as this will fool the plant into thinking it needs to reproduce, inducing roots to form. The best way to do this is to bend the shoot at right angles before burying it, to form an 'elbow'. However, in some cases (especially with more mature wood or when propagating roses, shown below) this isn't possible, so you'll need to restrict the supply in other ways. You can make a slanting cut in the shoot, about halfway through the wood; keep the cut open by inserting a small stick or stone in it. Alternatively, remove a piece of bark from the shoot, as described below.

Whichever method you use, dig a shallow hole in the soil or compost and, using a galvanized wire staple, peg the stem firmly in position in the hole so that it can't move in the wind, then cover the pinned-down part of the stem with soil. Water and leave it to root.

Other layering methods

Although simple layering works for most plants that are able to be propagated by layering, some need to be treated slightly differently.

Tip layering

Some plants, such as blackberries (*Rubus*) and its associated hybrids, including loganberries and tayberries, will root where their tips touch the ground, so you'll need to bury about 5cm (2in) of the stem-tip, pegging it down to prevent movement. If you're preparing tip layers for sale or giving away, dig a hole and bury a pot filled with compost, so you can layer the tip directly into the pot. When it has rooted you can sever the layer from the main plant and lift the pot.

Air layering

This technique is generally used when it isn't possible to lower a branch down to ground level. Unlike other forms of layering, it takes place on an aerial shoot (one higher up the plant) rather than on the ground.

HOW TO propagate by simple layering

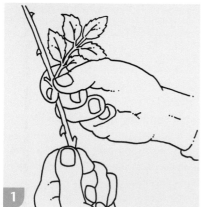

1 Choose a flexible shoot (here, a rose) that will bend down to the ground. About 30–40cm (12–16in) or so from the end of the shoot, remove the leaves and cut 5cm (2in) of bark from the underside, using a sharp knife, to a depth of only 1–2mm (¹/₁₆in). Take care not to sever the shoot.

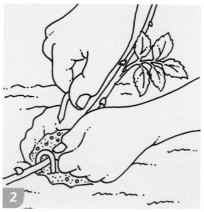

2 Bend the shoot onto the ground. Where the wounded part touches the soil, break up the ground beneath with a trowel or hand fork and make a shallow depression. Anchor the shoot into the depression by pegging it down using a looped piece of stout, galvanized wire.

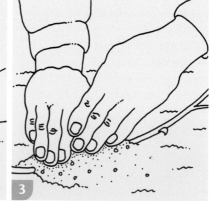

3 Cover the layered stem with soil, then water it thoroughly and leave it to root. This will usually take about three months. Detach the new shoot from the parent plant, cutting just before the layer. Pot up the new plant or transplant it directly to its new location.

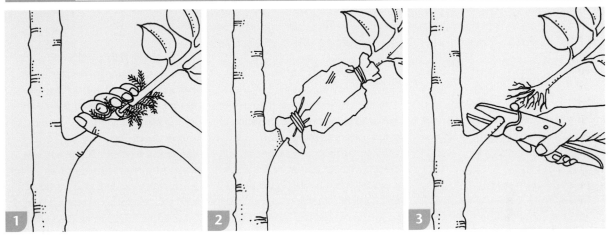

1 Choose a straight, healthy branch. Trim off any sideshoots to leave about 30cm (12in) of clear stem. About 23cm (9in) from the tip, remove a band of bark about 1cm (½in) wide from around the stem. Pack damp sphagnum moss around the 'wound'.

2 Wrap the stem and sphagnum moss in a piece of black polythene, tying it round the stem both above and below the layer to seal it. The plastic will protect the layer and prevent algal growth. Leave the plastic in place for about a year, checking occasionally for signs of rooting.

3 When strong new roots have formed, remove the plastic sleeve. Cut through the plant's stem just below the rootball to detach the layer from the parent plant. Pot up the new plant, or plant it straight into the garden in well-prepared soil. Water thoroughly and label.

First, 'wound' the stem (*see* above), then wrap the wound in damp sphagnum moss and cover with polythene. Leave the layer for about a year to root, then sever the young plant from its parent.

This method is successful for many climbers and shrubs, including magnolias, witch hazels (*Hamamelis*), daphnes and rhododendrons. Ideally, plants are layered in spring for replanting in autumn or the following spring.

Mass layering

A number of ericaceous plants, such as heaths (*Erica*), heathers (*Calluna*), vacciniums and cassiopes, lend themselves to a very easy method of mass production. Clip the plant all over to induce new growth, and when this is produced in spring, simply bury the plant in fibrous compost so that only the tips of the shoots are showing. You can do this by digging up the plant and then reburying it in a deep hole, or simply piling compost onto the plant as it is (this may wash off, so check after rain). The next autumn, lift the plant, cut off all the rooted shoots and pot them up.

Aftercare and replanting

It pays to give the new young plant some attention. Try to keep the area around the layer slightly damp. After a month or so, you can remove the growing-tip so that the shoot above the layer starts to branch out. Once roots have formed, the layer can be severed from the main plant and potted up or planted out in its final position in the garden.

Magnolias, especially the slower-growing ones like *M. stellata* (here, 'Rosea'), are suited to air layering.

Division

Division is one of the mainstays of propagation. In fact, it is one of the mainstays of gardening, because even if you don't want any new plants, a great number need to be regularly divided to prevent them from becoming overcrowded and dwindling in flower power. Some shrubby plants can be divided, but it is usually perennials that are increased by division.

In the wild, division naturally occurs when a plant is disturbed by animals digging, by landslips or by water eroding away the soil around the plant and breaking it into pieces. However, in the garden it involves dividing a plant into two or more sections, which form new plants.

As with all vegetative methods of propagation, division means that you can create a new plant that is identical to the parent. It is a quick and easy method, with new plants being created far more quickly than by taking cuttings or growing from seed. Indeed, if the plant sections are sufficiently large they can be planted straight back into the soil in the open garden.

Dividing perennials

There are different ways to divide perennials, from chopping the plant in half to carefully separating parts of the plant so that none of the roots is damaged. The plant you're intending to divide needs to have two or more crowns (pieces of plant, each with a growth bud and roots), and you're aiming to end up with smaller pieces, each with some roots and at least one or two promising

What plants can be divided and when?

Most perennials can be divided. Those that are mat-forming, such as asters, are usually the easiest, but any plant with multiple crowns can usually be divided. Generally, it's best to avoid plants that have a single rosette and/or are tap-rooted (with a large, single root that grows straight down into the soil rather than spreading out over a wide area). Some of these can be divided, but it takes experience to get them to survive. Plants in the following genera can sometimes be difficult to divide: *Aquilegia, Dianthus, Erysimum, Hieraceum, Oenothera, Papaver* and *Pulsatilla*. They are usually obvious to the eye because of their compact growth.

Early spring is the best time to divide most plants. At this time, plants are just starting into growth but haven't yet got a lot of foliage to sap their strength while the roots are still recovering. Autumn is fine for dividing the tougher, fibrous-rooted plants, such as Michaelmas daisies (*Aster novi-belgii*), but is not good for fleshy-rooted plants such as sedums and hostas. Bulbs are best divided when dormant (*see* page 60).

Dividing plants (here, kniphofia) is a quick, easy way to make new plants for free if you have space to fill in a border. Also, it will rejuvenate the clump.

shoots. Throw away the central, unproductive part.

Dividing with a spade

The simplest and quickest method involves digging the plant out of the ground, taking care not to damage the roots, placing it on the surface of the soil and simply chopping the plant in half with a sharp spade (*see* below). You can then either replant the two halves in prepared soil, or repeat the process, using a spade or sharp knife to make smaller pieces.

Easy to divide	
Aster	Iris sibirica
Anaphalis	Nepeta
Geranium	Rudbeckia
Helleborus	Sanguisorba
Hemerocallis	Veronica

Remember, the smaller they get, the more roots you lose.

This method works well for large divisions of resilient perennials and plants with tough rootstocks that form a single, woody mass, such as hostas, astilbes, agapanthus, delphiniums, hellebores, peonies, rheums and helianthus. Since roots can be damaged easily, disease can get into the new plant, so it's not something to try on rare or precious plants or those with more delicate root systems.

Two-fork method

Again, dig up the plant and place it on the surface of the soil. Insert two forks near the centre of the plant, so that the tines are back to back, and press the handles together so that the tines of the fork move apart,

One division method is to push two forks, back to back, into the clump and push the handles together.

HOW TO divide clumps using a spade

1 If it hasn't rained recently, water the clump (here, *Hosta*), then cut round it with a spade. Gently work the whole thing free and lift it out of the ground.

2 Where the roots divide naturally, slice through the clump with a sharp spade or knife to split it into smaller pieces, each with some roots.

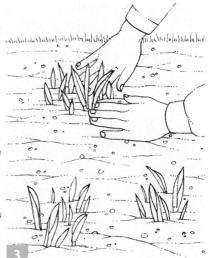

3 Plant each piece in well-prepared ground, firm the soil and water in. You can pot up some smaller pieces as spares. Don't delay or the plants may dry out.

gradually separating the plant into two. Repeat the process, making the portions smaller and smaller.

This technique works reasonably well when the soil is crumbly, as it pulls the roots apart, but if the soil is at all heavy the roots can break up as the two halves separate, again leaving the possibility of infection getting into the plant.

It is a good method for plants that have looser rootstocks, including day lilies (*Hemerocallis*), asters,

chrysanthemums, geraniums, penstemons, ornamental grasses and echinaceas.

Hand method

The hand method takes a bit more time, but is kinder to the plant than the other two methods, and you'll end up with many more healthy divisions with hardly anything wasted. It is a particularly good method for plants that have loose rootstocks and form smaller, low-growing clumps, such as primulas, heucheras, snowdrops (*Galanthus*) and pulmonarias.

First, dig up the plant; if the soil is soft and crumbly, shake the plant to

Dividing for health

Many perennials need dividing to keep them healthy, even if you don't want to propagate them to create more plants. They will frequently die out from the middle, so always use the younger growth round the edge of the plant for replanting or propagation. Plants that benefit from regular division are *Achillea*, *Aster*, *Delphinium*, *Phlox*, *Schizostylis* and bearded irises. However, others will go on for many years if left undisturbed, so you can just leave them unless you want to make more plants. The latter group includes *Acanthus*, *Aconitum*, *Agapanthus*, *Alchemilla*, *Alstroemeria*, *Anemone*, *Gypsophila*, *Helleborus*, *Hemerocallis*, *Iris unguicularis*, *Liriope*, *Nepeta*, *Paeonia*, *Papaver orientale*, *Pulsatilla* and *Tellima*.

remove all the soil, then with slight manipulation of the fingers separate the various crowns into individual plants. Try it with primulas, and the individual parts seem to come apart as if by magic. For heavier soils, immerse the plant in water and, again, manipulate it with your fingers. As the soil comes off, the pieces become easier to pull apart.

Replanting the divisions

Plant larger divisions in small groups, first giving the soil a boost with compost. Smaller pieces can be potted up in individual pots filled with John Innes No. 3 compost or general or multipurpose potting compost. Place them in a shaded cold frame if you have one for a few days until they've settled down, then harden them off (*see* page 20). Do not let them dry out. When they are happily growing, they're ready to plant out or give away.

The safest way to divide plants is to use your hands, as you're less likely to damage the plant's roots.

Other types of division

Plants that produce offsets or spread by underground runners, stolons or rhizomes are treated slightly differently from other perennials.

Offsets

Some plants, particularly bulbs (*see* pages 60–1 and below), succulents (*see* page 43) and some indoor plants, including bromeliads, develop small plants around their edges. These are usually complete plants and can be separated easily and potted up or planted outdoors, just as you would any young plant.

Grape hyacinths (*Muscari*) produce small offsets (or 'bulblets') around the parent bulb.

Runners

Runners are stems that spread out from the parent plant and root at intervals, producing new plants. The example that most gardeners know is the strawberry. Other examples are *Ajuga* and herbaceous *Potentilla*. These runners can be allowed to root in the soil around the parent plant and then the new plants can be dug up once they've formed.

Strawberry runners are pinned into compost-filled pots and left to form new young plantlets.

Alternatively, the runner can be pinned down, or 'layered' into pots filled with compost so ready-potted plants are formed (*see* above).

Suckers and stolons

Quite a number of shrubs and a few herbaceous plants form suckers and stolons, sometimes to the point of being a nuisance, as is the case with the shrub *Rhus* or the weed couch grass (*Elytrigia repens*).

Suckers are roots that travel some way from the parent plant and then throw up a new plant. These can be divided by cutting through the connecting root and then either planting out or potting up.

Stolons are underground stems rather than roots, but they're treated in the same way as suckers. Often the stolon can be dug up and transplanted without a new plant being already formed. *Corydalis* and mint are good examples of this.

Corydalis elata forms small stolons that spread underground, producing more plants.

Rhizomes

Some plants form thick stems that travel along the ground. Flag irises and *Iris germanica* are familiar examples. A whole section of these can be cut away from the parent plant and replanted. Alternatively, thick rhizomes can be cut into sections as long as each has a growing point (bud) and is potted up and kept in a propagator until new roots have formed and the bud starts to grow, producing leaves.

The roots (suckers) of *Agave americana* 'Variegata' produce rosettes that can be removed and potted up.

Bulbs

Many of the common bulbs are so inexpensive it may seem unnecessary to propagate your own, but it's enjoyable and satisfying, and fun to experiment. For less common bulbs that aren't available from commercial sources, you may have no option but to try. Usually, a bulb will have at least two ways of increasing. It's worth noting that the term 'bulbs' here includes corms and tubers as well as true bulbs. (*See also* box, page 62.)

Like all crocusus, *C. tommasinianus* 'Whitewell Purple' produces offsets that are easy to remove and replant.

Division

One of the simplest and quickest ways of increasing established clumps of bulbs is by division. The best time is when they're dormant, just after growth dies down and the roots become inactive. Use a garden fork to lift the whole clump, taking care not to damage the outer bulbs. Divide the bulbs into several smaller clumps by teasing the roots apart with your hands (*see* page 58) or using two forks (*see* pages 57–8). Pull off any dead leaves and roots, loose outer skin and shrivelled or diseased bulbs. Then replant the new clumps at the appropriate distances and depths after adding a blood, fish and bonemeal fertilizer.

Taking offsets

Bulbs often produce offsets around the parent bulb (*see* box, below, opposite, and page 59). If the bulb is lifted, these offsets can be removed and potted up individually or planted in the ground, and will grow into an exact replica of the parent plant. The process is very simple.

Some bulbous plants, such as lilies (*Lilium*) and alliums, produce little bulbs (bulbils) in the axils of the leaves (where the leaf or leaf-stalk joins the main stem), as shown below. These bulbils are ready when they come away easily if rubbed with the fingers. They can be 'sown'

Don't forget

Division is not only for propagation purposes. If bulbs multiply too much below ground, forming a tight clump of plants, they will lose vigour, producing prolific foliage but few flowers. For this reason, it's important to divide clumps of many plants to ensure their vitality.

Bulbs to propagate by offsets

Allium	*Iris*
Alstroemeria	*Leucojum*
Arum	*Lilium*
Crinum	*Muscari*
Crocus	*Narcissus*
Fritillaria	*Nerine*
Galanthus	*Ornithogalum*
Gladiolus	*Tulipa*

Don't forget

Always replant divided bulbs immediately in order to prevent them drying out, adding fertilizer to the soil as you do so.

Offsets of different bulb types

Many bulbs produce offspring above or below ground in the natural course of their growth cycle. These can be removed and replanted; each juvenile offset will grow into an exact replica of its parent.

CORMLETS (*Gladiolus*)

BULBLETS (*Narcissus*)

BULBILS (*Allium*)

BULBILS (*Lilium*)

HOW TO propagate from offsets

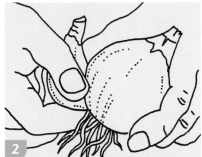

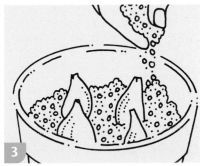

1 Dig up the parent bulbs with a fork while they are dormant or (in the case of gladioli) when the foliage is dying back. Gently shake or brush off any excess soil onto a sheet or tray.

2 Carefully pull offsets from the parent bulb, which can then be replanted (*see* Step 3) or dried for storage. Check the loose excess soil for any offsets you may have overlooked.

3 Plant offsets in pots or trays of moist, gritty potting compost immediately or in spring, about 2.5cm (1in) apart and deep. Grow on in an unheated greenhouse or bulb frame for 1–2 years before planting out.

in the same way as seed: lay them on top of a pot of compost and cover them with a thin layer of horticultural grit. Sow them straightaway, as they will dry out if you store them too long.

Bulbils are not confined to bulbs. Some herbaceous perennials, for instance *Cardamine bulbifera*, also produce them and are treated in exactly the same way.

Sowing seed

You don't necessarily think of seed in connection with bulbs, but in fact it's the best way to introduce new bulbs to your collection, and is the safest way to propagate new stock

Bulbs to propagate by seed

Chionodoxa (dwarf and miniature)	*Galanthus*
	Narcissus
Crocus	*Iris reticulata*
Cyclamen	*Sisyrinchium*
Eranthis	*Tulipa*

free from most diseases (other methods pass on the health status of the parents).

A drawback of sowing seed is that it may not produce an exact replica of the parent. However, there is of course the possibility of growing something new and interesting – indeed, nearly all the hundreds of variations that are avidly collected by enthusiasts have come about by either accidental or deliberate propagation from seed.

Most bulb seed should be sown fresh, as soon as it is collected (*see* pages 24–8). Some hardy bulbs, especially spring-flowering kinds, such as daffodils and fritillaries, need a period of dormancy before they germinate, so you'll need to keep them outdoors or in a cold frame after sowing. Bulbs do not

Don't forget

Hybrids of many bulbs are sterile and therefore do not set seed. The only way to know if they're sterile is by experience and observation.

develop as quickly as other plants, and it's often necessary to leave the young seedlings in their pot for at least two years before potting on. They will grow more quickly if you can keep them in growth for as long as possible, so don't let them dry out while they have leaves showing, but stop watering as soon as the young bulbs go dormant.

Other techniques

The most common ways of propagating bulbs are by division or sowing seed. However, if you become hooked on bulbs there will inevitably come a time when you want to propagate a rare bulb that neither sets seed nor readily produces offsets, or you may simply want to speed up the process or produce a lot of new plants from a single bulb. In these cases, you'll have to turn to a vegetative method such as scooping, scoring or scaling (*see* page 62). Before starting work, you must sterilize all pots and tools.

Corms and tubers

You'll often see corms and tubers grouped together with bulbs at the garden centre or in bulb catalogues. Although they are similar – all are underground storage organs – they do differ from a botanical point of view and there are some differences in how they're propagated.

Crocuses, freesias, crocosmias and gladioli are all examples of corms (condensed stems). All can be treated in the same way as bulbs when it comes to planting and growing, and, like bulbs, corms can be raised from seed or offsets (known as 'cormlets' or 'cormels'). However, you can also divide corms. Take a healthy corm at normal planting time and cut it into sections, each containing at

least one bud. Coat the cut surfaces with fungicide and put to one side for a couple of days in a warm place. Once the cut surfaces have dried, plant either in the ground or in pots as you would for individual bulbs.

Tubers are modified roots (for example, dahlias) or underground stems (such as potatoes). Although both can be grown from seed, we tend to want a particular variety, so a vegetative process is the only way to ensure this. In the case of dahlias, after their winter dormancy cut off the individual tubers, ensuring each piece has a bud on it, and pot them up in early spring. Alternatively, take basal cuttings in early spring (see page 38).

In the case of potatoes, the very action of harvesting is a form of division, and come the following spring you can replant individuals. Alternatively, cut a potato into thick slices, each with a bud on it, and plant as you would a whole potato – you'll end up with several potato plants from one tuber.

Scooping and scoring

A number of common bulbs can be increased by methods known as scooping and scoring, particularly hyacinths (*Hyacinthus*), which can be reluctant to multiply by other methods. Daffodils (*Narcissus*) and snowdrops (*Galanthus*) can also be reproduced in the same way. Both methods are carried out at the end of the bulbs' dormant period.

For scooping, use a sterile knife or teaspoon to remove the inner part of the basal plate. For scoring, make two V-shaped grooves at right angles to each other in the bulb's base. Dust the cut bulb with fungicide and set it upside down in a dish of dry sand in a warm, dry place while the cuts callus over, then moisten the sand. When bulblets appear, plant the whole bulb upside down in a pot of compost which just covers the bulblets. Place the bulblets in a propagator and leave until they are big enough to pot up separately.

Scaling

Scaling is a method that is used to increase bulbs surrounded by scales, particularly lilies (*Lilium*) but also fritillaries (*Fritillaria*). Collect lilies for

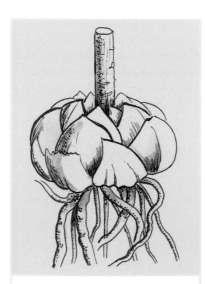

Lily bulbs are covered in scales. If removed and put in compost, they will produce new plants.

scaling in late summer or early autumn, before root growth starts, and scale them straight away. Remove a few of the outer scales by snapping them off as close as possible to the base of the bulb to retain a small piece of basal tissue. Dust thoroughly with fungicide, then place them in a polythene bag that has been half filled with damp vermiculite or sterile compost. Seal the bag and place it in a warm, shaded place until young bulblets begin to appear at the base of the scales. Plant each scale into compost, burying the bulblets, and put them into a propagator until the bulblets have developed sufficiently to be divided and planted up into pots on their own.

Twin scaling

Twin scaling is a popular way of producing large numbers of snowdrops from a single bulb, and this method can also be used for daffodils and hyacinths.

Cut up a healthy snowdrop soon after it becomes dormant into as many segments as you can, each piece having a section of basal plate. Peel back the scales of each segment, two at a time, and cut down through the basal plate to remove these two scales so each pair retains a small piece of basal plate. After dusting the twin scales with fungicide, treat them in the same way as single scales (see above). When you are twin scaling, all equipment must be absolutely sterile or failure will result.

Don't forget

If cormlets are small and have dried out over winter, soak them in water before planting out.

Grafting

Propagating can become addictive, and success can bring on the desire for more challenges. The most common propagation methods used by gardeners have already been described, but there are some other techniques, including grafting, that are used when plants are difficult to increase by seed or cuttings, or if many plants are required. These more advanced techniques tend to belong to the realm of specialists, but some are within the capabilities of a skilled amateur gardener.

What is grafting?

Grafting is used mainly to propagate trees and shrubs, although some herbaceous plants can be increased this way too. A cutting (known as a scion) is taken from the plant you want to propagate and it is grafted onto the roots and bit of stem (the rootstock) of another similar, but easy-to-grow plant. The advantage of grafting is that you can produce a large number of plants from one individual, and can control the size and increase the vigour of the plant by careful selection of the rootstock: something that cannot be done by any other method.

These four-year-old spruces (*Picea*) were grafted at the nursery onto dwarf rootstocks to create neat, compact standard trees. The graft union is visible on the stem.

The rootstock will determine many of the characteristics of a grafted plant. It can restrict the size of very vigorous varieties, provide strength to weak growers, and even help with disease resistance.

In the case of many ornamental trees and shrubs, including roses, the rootstock is a common species that has been grown from seed. With fruit trees, the rootstock is selected from specially raised plants that will have a bearing on the height, vigour or ability of the tree to grow in particular conditions. It can also enable trees to fruit at a younger age than they might do naturally.

For example, in the case of apples there are six main named rootstocks. At one end of the spectrum, M27 produces a very small tree (about 2–3m/6–10ft at maturity), while M25 becomes extremely large and vigorous; the other rootstocks are somewhere in between. To ensure you end up with an appropriate tree suited to the size of your garden, it's essential to choose the right rootstock.

Several different apple or pear varieties can be grafted one above the other onto an existing mature tree, resulting in a 'family tree' (*see* page 65).

Many plants you buy at the garden centre or nursery will already have been grafted, particularly fruit trees and roses; you can tell because there is usually a clear ridge or bump on the stem just above soil level.

The disadvantage of grafted plants is that rootstocks are liable to produce their own shoots, known as suckers, which compete with the desired plant if they aren't removed.

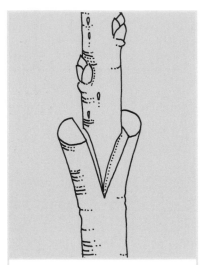

To wedge graft, make a vertical cut about 3cm (1in) long down through the stem of the rootstock. Cut both sides of the base of the scion to form a wedge, or V-shape. Gently push the wedge down into the slit in the rootstock and bind with grafting tape as for whip-and-tongue grafting.

Grafting techniques

There are numerous grafting techniques, some of which are fairly straightforward, provided you have a steady hand, a sharp knife and the know-how. To ensure success, the scion (the piece you are grafting onto the rootstock) and rootstock need to be a very similar size so they can fit together tightly, and the angles at which they are cut need to match, or the graft won't take.

The easiest and most common methods of grafting are whip-and-tongue grafting (*see* below) and wedge grafting (*see* left). Both are suitable for propagating woody plants, but whip-and-tongue tends to be used mainly for fruit trees and wedge grafting for ornamental trees and shrubs. Although they sound complicated, with practice they will become easier to accomplish.

Saddle grafting is almost the reverse of wedge grafting: a wedge is cut on the rootstock, the scion is cut in an inverted V-shape, and the two pieces are then fitted together in the same way as for wedge grafting. The techniques can be used interchangeably for the same plants.

How to graft

Whether you're whip-and-tongue or wedge grafting, the preparatory stages are the same.

A year before you want to make the graft, plant the rootstock where you want the plant to grow so it can become established. It can grow either in the ground or in a pot, but

Don't forget

Avoid touching any cut surfaces with your fingers, as you could contaminate the cambium, causing disease.

HOW TO whip-and-tongue graft

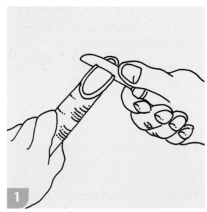
1

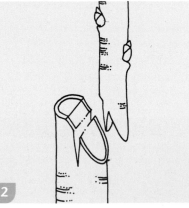
2

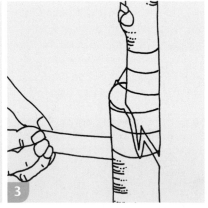
3

First, prepare the rootstock that you planted the previous year. Using a sharp knife, make an upward-sloping cut. About one third of the way down this, make a vertical, V-shaped cut about 1cm (½in) deep into the stem (*see* step 2). This forms a 'tongue', which will connect to a similar one on the scion.

At the base of the scion, create a mirror image of the cut that you made on the rootstock, first making a sloping cut through the stem (with a bud just above the base of the cut), then making a vertical cut. Join the two parts together, so that the tongue of the rootstock slides neatly into the notch in the scion.

Bind the graft firmly with a clear plastic tape or grafting tape, at least 2.5cm (1in) above and below the area where the two pieces are joined together. When the two have callused over and have become united, remove the tape. Once the new tree starts to grow, remove any shoots, or 'suckers', that appear on the rootstock.

in both cases the soil or compost should not be too wet.

The following winter, cut the scion from a healthy shoot of the previous year's growth. If you can't graft straightaway, heel it into well-drained soil until it is required.

Grafting should be carried out in late winter or early spring. Before you begin, make a horizontal cut across the top of the rootstock, shortening it to about 25cm (10in), and trim off any sideshoots. Cut the scion, reducing it to about three or four buds and removing any soft growth at the tip. The length of the scion should be about 15cm (6in). Next, follow the instructions shown according to whether you're whip-and-tongue grafting or wedge grafting (*see* opposite).

Malus 'Coronet' is a prime example of a grafted specimen. It contains two varieties of apple (hence being called a 'family tree') and remains miniature all its life.

Suitable for grafting

Aesculus	Hamamelis
Caragana	Hibiscus
Catalpa	Malus
Cercis	Prunus
Citrus	Pyrus
Daphne	Rhododendron
Fagus	Robinia
Fraxinus	Rosa
Gleditsia	Syringa

Micropropagation

Commercial plant breeders use an advanced technique known as micropropagation. In essence, the propagator takes a small piece of plant tissue, puts it into a culture and lets the cells multiply until tiny new plants are formed. It is a good way of rapidly increasing large quantities of highly bred or genetically modified plants that do not propagate easily from seed or by vegetative methods. However, it requires completely sterile, laboratory conditions and considerable scientific knowledge, so is beyond the scope of this book.

Once the tree or shrub has started to grow, remove any shoots that appear below the graft, as these will reflect the character of the rootstock and not the scion.

If you planted the rootstock in a container, keep it in a propagator or greenhouse until the union is strong, then plant the grafted tree or shrub into its final position in the garden.

Propagating roses

Commercial growers propagate roses by a method of grafting known as 'budding', which is the most reliable way to produce many plants that are all uniform in habit, of equal size and ready to sell at the same time. It is particularly useful for reproducing highly bred cultivars, such as hybrid teas (*Rosa* 'Freedom' shown right), which are unable to develop a strong root system and so benefit from being grafted onto a more vigorous rootstock.

The experienced gardener may want to try budding, but there are easier and quicker ways to propagate roses, as long as you're happy seeing more of the rose's individual peculiarities in terms of shapes, sizes and growth habits. All can be propagated by semi-ripe cuttings in spring or summer, either from the shoot tip or with a heel, or by hardwood cuttings in winter; roses with lax, spreading branches can be layered; and species roses grown for their hips and Rugosa roses can be grown from seed.

A–Z propagation directory

This directory contains most of the plants the average gardener is likely to encounter, including ornamental plants (*see* pages 67–87), and edible plants (*see* pages 88–91). All gardeners seem to differ in the way they propagate plants, and climatic conditions vary from year to year and place to place, so bear in mind that what follows is only a starting point, and you'll learn through experience what methods and timings work best for you.

Ornamental plants

Unless specifically mentioned, assume that no heat is required. Where gentle heat is referred to, set an electric propagator to a temperature a few degrees above the ambient temperature in a cold greenhouse, somewhere in the region of 16–18°C (61–64°F). Where fresh seed is specified, it means sow seed straight after it has been collected or, in the case of bought seed, order early and sow as soon as you have the packet in your hand.

PLANT	PROPAGATION METHODS
Abelia	Softwood or greenwood cuttings in summer or layering.
Abutilon	Softwood, greenwood or semi-ripe cuttings in spring or summer, hardwood cuttings in winter. Species from seed sown in spring.
Acacia (Mimosa, wattle)	Greenwood cuttings in summer. Seed sown in spring (soak seed before sowing).
Acanthus (Bear's breeches)	Easiest method is root cuttings in winter, although older plants can be divided, with difficulty, in spring. Species from seed sown in spring.
Acer (Maple)	Species from seed sown fresh (chilling the seed breaks dormancy). Softwood cuttings in spring or summer are difficult but possible.
Achillea (Yarrow)	Division in spring or autumn. Also basal cuttings taken in spring. Species from seed sown in autumn or spring.
Aconitum (Monkshood)	Division of tuberous roots in spring or autumn. Species from pre-chilled seed sown in spring. Tubers and seeds are poisonous.
Acorus (Sweet flag)	Division in spring.
Adiantum (Maidenhair fern)	Division in spring. Spores sown fresh.
Adonis (Pheasant's eye)	Annuals from seed sown in spring. Species from fresh seed in spring. Division with some difficulty in spring.
Aesculus (Horse chestnut)	Species from seed sown fresh. Varieties by grafting.
Agapanthus (African lily)	Division in spring. Species from seed sown in spring.
Agastache (Anise hyssop)	Short-lived, so best treated as an annual and grown from seed sown in spring. Can be divided in spring or propagated from basal cuttings in spring.
Agave (Century plant)	Many can be increased only from seed in gentle heat (hand-pollinate to get seed). Some produce offsets and others produce suckers that can be divided in spring.
Ageratum	Sow in 20–25°C (68–77°F) heat in spring.
Ajuga (Bugle)	Division in spring or autumn.
Alcea (Hollyhock)	Most suffer from rust, so although perennials they are best treated as annuals and grown from seed in spring, summer or autumn.
Alchemilla (Lady's mantle)	Easy from seed sown in autumn, often self-sowing. Mat-forming species such as *A. conjuncta* by division in spring.
Allium	Division of offsets in autumn. Sow seed or bulbils at the same time of year.
Alonsoa	Perennials usually treated as annuals, so grow from seed sown in spring.

PLANT	PROPAGATION METHODS
Alstroemeria (Peruvian lily)	Mainly seed sown in summer; put bag over seedheads to capture the seed. Division in autumn is possible but difficult as roots are brittle.
Althaea (Hollyhock)	Sow seed in autumn or spring.
Amaranthus (Love-lies-bleeding)	Sow in gentle heat in spring.
Amelanchier (Snowy mespilus)	Layering is one of the best methods, although those that produce suckers can be divided in spring.
Anaphalis (Pearly everlasting)	Division in spring.
Anchusa	Annuals and species from seed sown in summer or, preferably, autumn. Root cuttings of named varieties in winter.
Anemone (Windflower)	Seed for species sown as fresh as possible. Division in autumn for wood anemone (*A. nemorosa*) cultivars. Division in spring or root cuttings in winter for Japanese anemones (*A. hupehensis* var. *japonica*, *A.* × *hybrida*). Division of tuberous-rooted *A. pavonina* types in autumn.
Angelica	Seed sown in autumn or spring. Will self-sow.
Anthemis	Basal cuttings or tip cuttings in spring. Some will self-sow but may not come true.
Antirrhinum	Perennials usually treated as biennials and sown in spring or autumn. Can be sown direct outdoors. Take tip cuttings in spring or autumn of ones you want to keep.
Aquilegia (Columbine)	Mainly seed sown fresh. Some types come true, others vary. Mature plants can be divided in autumn or spring but it is not easy.
Arabis	Perennials come easily from tip cuttings in spring. Annuals from seed sown in spring.
Argyranthemum	Tip cuttings in spring or summer.
Artemisia	Basal cuttings in spring.
Arum	Seed sown fresh. They will often self-sow. Tubers of mature plants can be divided in summer.
Asplenium	Division in spring, sow spores when ripe or root bulbils.
Aster (Michaelmas daisy)	Fibrous-rooted, spreading types, such as *A. novae-angliae* and *A. novi-belgii*, can be easily divided in autumn or spring. Clump-forming types, such as *A.* × *frikartii*, are difficult to divide and should be increased by basal cuttings or tip cuttings in spring. Species from seed sown in spring.
Astilbe	Division in spring or autumn.
Astrantia	Division in spring or autumn.
Athyrium (Lady fern)	Division in spring, sow spores when ripe or root bulbils.
Aubrieta (Aubretia)	After flowering, shear over the plant and then take cuttings from the new growth that appears.

PLANT	PROPAGATION METHODS
Aucuba (Spotted laurel)	Semi-ripe cuttings in summer or from seed. Will also layer easily.
Ballota	Softwood or semi-ripe cuttings in summer.
Baptisia	Spring-sown seed, preferably soaked in warm water overnight. Mature plants can also be divided, but not always successfully as they resent disturbance.
Begonia	Seed is extremely fine and sowing difficult, unless mixed first with sand (*see* page 27). Germination needs gentle heat. Can also be propagated from leaf cuttings in the growing season.
Berberis (Barberry)	Semi-ripe cuttings (can be taken with a heel) in summer. Species can be grown from seed. Self-sown seedlings will not come true for named varieties.
Bergenia (Elephant's ears)	Seed sown in autumn or spring. Named varieties should be divided in spring or grown from cuttings of the thick rhizomes, ensuring that each section has a bud.
Betula (Birch)	Seed sown fresh. Softwood cuttings from spring to summer. Named varieties can be grafted.
Bidens	Annuals from seed sown in gentle heat in spring. Perennials can be divided in autumn or spring.
Blechnum (Hard fern)	Division in spring or sow spores when ripe.
Borago (Borage)	Seed sown outdoors in spring. Will self-sow.
Briza (Quaking grass)	Seed sown in spring.
Brunnera	Seed sown in spring or division in spring or autumn. Root cuttings in winter.
Buddleja (Buddleia)	Hardwood cuttings in autumn or winter. Will also come from softwood, greenwood and semi-ripe cuttings in summer. Self-sown seedlings do not come true.
Buxus (Box)	Semi-ripe cuttings in summer.
Calamintha	Tip cuttings in summer or division in spring. Will also propagate by seed sown in spring.
Calendula (Pot marigold)	Sow seed in pots or open ground in spring or autumn.
Caltha (Kingcup, marsh marigold)	Division after flowering. Can be propagated by fresh seed, but as it is a water-loving plant ensure the compost stays moist.
Camassia	Division after flowering or in autumn. Can also be propagated from seed, preferably sown fresh.
Camellia	Semi-ripe or leaf-bud cuttings in summer, or hardwood cuttings in autumn. Can also be propagated by layering or seed sown in autumn or spring (seed may need soaking to break dormancy).
Campanula (Bellflower)	Seed or division (named varieties only from the latter) in spring or autumn. Some can be increased by basal cuttings in spring.
Canna	Seed sown in gentle heat or division, both in spring.
Cardamine	Seed sown in spring or autumn, or division after flowering. *C. bulbifera* from bulbils sown fresh.

PLANT	PROPAGATION METHODS
Cardiocrinum	Seed sown fresh or division of offsets of mature bulbs in autumn.
Carex (Sedge)	Seed or division, both in spring.
Caryopteris	Semi-ripe cuttings in summer.
Catananche (Cupid's dart)	Seed sown in autumn or spring. Can also be increased by taking root cuttings in winter.
Ceanothus	Softwood, greenwood or semi-ripe cuttings in summer, or hardwood cuttings in winter.
Centaurea (Cornflower)	Annuals from seed sown in autumn or spring; can be sown in open ground. Perennials from division in spring. Some, such as *C. dealbata*, from root cuttings in winter.
Centranthus (Red valerian)	Root cuttings in spring or seed sown in autumn or spring; can be sown in open ground. Will self-sow.
Cephalaria	Seed or division in spring. Some, such as *C. gigantea*, can be increased by root cuttings in winter.
Cerastium (Snow-in-summer)	Seed or division in spring. Shear over the plant after flowering and take cuttings from new growth.
Ceratostigma	Softwood, greenwood or semi-ripe cuttings in summer. *C. plumbaginoides* can be divided in spring.
Cerinthe	Sow seed outdoors, preferably in spring but also in autumn in milder areas.
Chaenomeles (Ornamental quince)	Semi-ripe cuttings in summer or layering for the more difficult ones.
Chelone (Turtlehead)	Division or basal cuttings in spring. Species from seed sown in spring.
Choisya (Mexican orange blossom)	Softwood, greenwood or semi-ripe cuttings in summer.
Chrysanthemum	Basal cuttings in winter or spring from plants overwintered under cover, or tip cuttings in spring. Hardy forms can be divided in spring.
Cistus (Sun rose)	Softwood cuttings in summer.
Clarkia	Seed sown in autumn or spring, directly into the garden.
Clematis	A large genus with some easier to propagate than others. Most cultivars will root from softwood, greenwood, semi-ripe or leaf-bud cuttings in summer; stem cuttings should be internodal (*see* box, page 38). Herbaceous clematis can be increased from basal cuttings taken in spring and some can, with care, be divided. Cultivars can also be increased by layering. The species can be grown from seed. This should be sown fresh, as soon as it is ripe. Young clematis can suffer from wilt, so plant them 10cm (4in) below the level they were in the pots.
Cleome (Spider plant)	Seed sown in gentle heat in spring.
Clivia	Careful division in spring. Some produce offsets which can be divided. Sow seed in gentle heat in spring, though it takes several years to get flowering plants.

PLANT	PROPAGATION METHODS
Cobaea	Perennials usually treated as annuals; seed sown in gentle heat in spring.
Colchicum (Autumn crocus)	Division of bulbs in spring, when the leaves have died down, or immediately after flowering. Species from seed sown in autumn.
Consolida	Seed sown in autumn or spring, preferably direct into open ground.
Convallaria (Lily-of-the-valley)	Division at any time, but particularly immediately after flowering.
Cordyline (Cabbage palm)	Seed sown in spring or autumn in gentle heat is the easiest method. If suckers are produced, these can be divided.
Coreopsis (Tickseed)	Annuals and species from seed sown in spring. Perennials, especially named forms, can be divided in spring. Alternatively, take tip cuttings or basal cuttings in spring.
Cornus (Dogwood)	Semi-ripe cuttings in summer or hardwood cuttings in winter. Seed is slow to germinate; it should be sown fresh.
Cortaderia (Pampas grass)	Division in spring, although larger clumps will be difficult to divide.
Corydalis	Most can be grown from seed sown fresh. The bulbous varieties can be divided after the leaves die down and the mat- or clump-forming types are best divided in spring.
Corylus (Hazel)	Species from seed (hazelnuts) or by making layers or dividing rooted shoots from the base.
Cosmos	Annuals and species can be grown from seed in gentle heat in spring. Perennials can be increased from basal cuttings in spring.
Cotinus (Smoke bush)	Softwood cuttings in summer or layering.
Cotoneaster	Softwood, greenwood or semi-ripe cuttings in summer. Seed sown fresh or in spring for species only. Can also be propagated by layering.
Crambe	Root cuttings in winter. (For *C. maritima*, *see* Sea kale, page 91.)
Crassula	Divide offsets, take stem or leaf cuttings, or sow seed from spring to summer.
Crepis (Hawk's beard)	Seed sown fresh or in spring. Root cuttings can be taken in winter and some respond to careful division in spring.
Crinum	Division of bulbs in spring is the best method. They can be grown from seed sown in spring, but take a long time to reach flowering size.
Crocosmia (Montbretia)	Division in spring. Species from seed sown in spring.
Crocus	Division in autumn. Species from seed sown in summer, especially *C. tommasinianus*, which self-sows prolifically.
Cyclamen	The easiest method is growing from seed sown from summer to winter (the seed needs soaking first to break dormancy). However, named varieties can be propagated by cutting the tubers into sections, each with a bud, in summer.
Cynara (Cardoon)	Division in spring or root cuttings in winter.

PLANT	PROPAGATION METHODS
Cypella	Division of bulbs and bulbils when dormant. Seed sown when ripe.
Cytisus (Broom)	Semi-ripe cuttings in summer. Self-sown seedlings will probably not come true unless they are species. Scarifying seed before sowing will help to break dormancy.
Dactylorhiza (Spotted orchid)	Division in summer or autumn. Difficult to grow from seed but self-sows easily.
Dahlia	Division of dormant tubers in winter, ensuring each has a bud. Basal cuttings in spring. Species from seed sown in gentle heat, preferably fresh.
Daphne	Species from seed sown when ripe in summer (ideally, pre-chill seeds before sowing). Most types propagate from softwood, greenwood or semi-ripe cuttings, although some are difficult to root. Layering or grafting are generally used for more difficult ones.
Delphinium	Basal or tip cuttings in spring. With care, it is possible to divide mature plants in spring. Species from seed sown fresh.
Deutzia	Softwood, greenwood or semi-ripe cuttings in spring or summer, or hardwood cuttings in autumn or winter.
Dianthus (Carnation, pink)	Species, annuals or those treated as biennials, such as sweet williams (*D. barbatus*), from seed sown in spring, summer or autumn. Named varieties by tip cuttings from non-flowering shoots in summer.
Diascia	Propagate easily from basal, tip or stem cuttings in spring or summer. Some gardeners find they come more easily from internodal cuttings.
Dicksonia (Tree fern)	Sow spores or sever offsets from trunks.
Dictamnus (Burning bush, dittany)	Seed sown fresh if possible. The seed capsules are explosive, so enclose in a bag to capture seed. Plants can be divided in spring with care.
Dierama (Angel's fishing rod)	Seed sown in spring. Alternatively, by careful division in spring.
Digitalis (Foxglove)	Annuals, biennials and species from seed sown in spring. Most self-sow. Clump-forming types by division in spring. Also, can be propagated from basal cuttings in spring.
Dipsacus (Teasel)	From seed sown in autumn or spring.
Doronicum (Leopard's bane)	Division in spring after flowering or in autumn.
Dryopteris (Buckler fern)	Division in spring or sow spores when ripe.
Eccremocarpus Chilean glory flower	These are perennial climbers that are often treated as annuals and grown from seed. Seed needs light to germinate, so best not covered with compost.
Echeveria	Separate and plant offsets and take leaf cuttings.
Echinacea	Basal cuttings or root cuttings in spring. Species can be increased from seed sown in spring.
Echinops (Globe thistle)	Division in spring is possible, but root cuttings in winter are easier. Species can be increased from seed sown in spring. They often self-sow.

PLANT	PROPAGATION METHODS
Echium	Most are biennials or monocarpic (die after flowering) and should be grown from seed. Perennials can be increased by tip cuttings in spring.
Elaeagnus	Semi-ripe cuttings in summer or hardwood cuttings in autumn or winter.
Epilobium (Willow herb)	Sow seed in spring, but don't cover seed too deeply as it needs light. Perennials can be divided in spring. Take tip cuttings of *E. glabellum* in autumn.
Epimedium	Most come easily from division in spring or autumn. Species can be grown from seed sown fresh.
Epipactis	As with most orchids, these are difficult to grow from seed but, if large enough, can be carefully divided in spring.
Eranthis (Winter aconite)	The tuberous rhizomes can be divided after flowering. They also come readily from seed if sown fresh.
Eremurus (Foxtail lily)	Divide crowns after their foliage has died down. Non-named varieties from seed sown in summer, but it can take up to six years to reach flowering size.
Erica (Heather)	Semi-ripe cuttings, preferably with a heel, taken in summer. Bury the plant in compost to layer the shoots – a technique known as mass layering (*see* page 55).
Erigeron (Fleabane)	Division or basal cuttings, both in spring. Also from seed sown in spring. *E. karvinskianus* produces plenty of self-sown seedlings.
Erodium (Storksbill)	Basal cuttings in spring. From seed sown fresh, though it may not come true.
Eryngium (Sea holly)	For named varieties, root cuttings in autumn or winter is the best way. For all others, sowing seed fresh or in spring works well. Plants can also be divided in spring.
Erysimum (Wallflower)	Perennial wallflowers can be readily increased by taking cuttings in spring or summer. The wallflowers usually treated as biennials (formerly *Cheiranthus*) are sown in spring for transplanting in autumn and flowering in the next year. Attractive forms can be kept going by taking tip cuttings in summer.
Erythronium (Dog's-tooth violet)	These bulbs can be readily increased by division. Most will propagate by seed, preferably sown fresh, but can take up to five years to flower.
Escallonia	Softwood or semi-ripe cuttings in summer.
Eschscholzia (California poppy)	Short-lived perennials that are usually treated as annuals and grown from seed sown in spring.
Eucomis (Pineapple flower)	Division in autumn or winter, when dormant. Can also be grown from seed sown in spring.
Eucryphia (Brush bush)	Semi-ripe cuttings in summer.
Euonymus	Softwood cuttings in summer. Some varieties may root more easily by layering. Sow seed in autumn (pre-chilling seed will help break dormancy).
Eupatorium (Hemp agrimony)	Division in autumn or spring. Sow seed fresh or in spring.
Euphorbia (Spurge)	Species of this large genus (over 2,000 species) from seed sown fresh if possible, those seeds with hard coatings benefiting from a soaking in water overnight.

PLANT	PROPAGATION METHODS
Euphorbia (continued)	Clump-forming types can be divided in spring. Many of the woodier forms can be increased from tip cuttings, while some come from sideshoots. The sap can be an irritant to the skin and is very painful in the eyes.
Exochorda	Softwood cuttings in summer or from layers.
Filipendula (Meadowsweet)	Division in spring or autumn is easy. Species can also be grown from seed sown fresh or in spring.
Foeniculum (Fennel)	Seedlings come readily from freshly sown seed. Will self-sow freely, but move seedlings quickly as they develop deep tap roots. Root cuttings in spring.
Forsythia	Softwood, greenwood or semi-ripe cuttings in summer. Hardwood cuttings in autumn. Also layering.
Francoa (Bridal wreath)	Division, basal cuttings or seed sown in spring.
Fraxinus (Ash)	Seed sown in autumn (pre-chilling will help to break dormancy).
Fremontodendron (Fremontia)	Softwood, greenwood or semi-ripe cuttings in spring. The hairs can be an irritant.
Fritillaria (Fritillary)	Like most bulbs, these can be divided while they are dormant. Seed is also an easy way of propagation, although it may take several years to get a flowering bulb.
Fuchsia	Softwood, greenwood or semi-ripe cuttings in summer.
Gaillardia (Blanket flower)	Sow seed in gentle heat in spring, or in the open ground when the soil has warmed up. Division of plants in spring. Root cuttings can be taken for perennial species in winter.
Galanthus (Snowdrop)	Division of bulbs in the dormant season is the easiest method. Twin scaling (*see* page 62) can also be used. Species can be increased from seed sown fresh.
Galega (Goat's rue)	Division of plants in autumn or spring. Basal cuttings in spring. Can be grown from seed in spring and will self-sow.
Garrya	Semi-ripe cuttings in summer.
Gaura	Generally raised from seed, but named varieties are best taken as summer cuttings. With care, older plants can be divided.
Gazania	Tender perennials that can be increased from summer cuttings and overwintered under cover. Can also be grown from seed sown in gentle heat in spring.
Genista (Broom)	Softwood, greenwood or semi-ripe cuttings taken in spring or summer. Self-sown seedlings may not come true.
Gentiana (Gentian)	Seed sown fresh or in spring after chilling. Seeds need light to germinate, so don't cover. Clump-forming varieties can be divided in spring and cuttings can be taken from many types, also in spring.
Geranium (Cranesbill)	A very large genus and most propagation methods can be used. Seed capsules are explosive, so need covering with bags to capture the contents. Resulting seed can be sown fresh or in spring. Named varieties need vegetative methods. Clump-forming varieties can be divided in autumn or spring. Some geraniums, for example *G. cinereum*, produce good cutting material in spring.

PLANT	PROPAGATION METHODS
Geum	Named varieties are best divided in spring. Species can be grown from seed sown fresh or in spring.
Gladiolus	Divide the bulbs when they are lifted in autumn. Species can be grown from seed sown fresh.
Glaucidium	Careful division is the best method of increase. They can also be grown from freshly sown seed, but take several years to reach flowering size.
Gunnera	Division is the best way, but it can be tricky for the largest species. Seed sown fresh is easier, but it takes much longer to get a mature plant.
Gypsophila (Baby's breath)	Seed sown in spring is the easiest method. Cuttings taken in spring work well for some forms (such as *G. paniculata*), but others may require root cuttings taken in winter. Some really difficult forms may need grafting on *G. paniculata* stock.
Hacquetia	Seed sown fresh. Seedlings are prone to damping off, so do not cover too tightly. Occasionally self-sows.
Hakonechloa	As with all grasses, this is best divided in spring.
Hamamelis (Witch hazel)	Grafting onto *H. virginiana* which comes from seed.
Hebe	Semi-ripe cuttings in summer or autumn.
Hedera (Ivy)	Remove natural layers. Semi-ripe cuttings in summer.
Helenium (Sneezeweed)	Division in spring or autumn. Basal cuttings or seed sown in spring.
Helianthemum (Rock rose)	Generally come readily from semi-ripe cuttings in summer.
Helianthus (Sunflower)	The annuals and species are grown from seed sown in spring. Perennial clumps can be easily increased by division in spring or autumn.
Helichrysum	Annuals or the perennial varieties treated as annuals are grown from seed sown in spring. Perennial forms are increased by tip cuttings in summer or autumn, but do not cover pots or trays closely or the cuttings will rot. Clump-forming plants divide easily in spring.
Helleborus (Hellebore)	All but named varieties propagate easily from seed, but only if sown fresh; old seed germinates poorly. Named varieties can be divided in spring after flowering.
Hemerocallis (Day lily)	Division in spring or autumn is the normal means of increase. Species can be grown from seed sown in spring, preferably with a bit of pre-chilling.
Hepatica	Division of named varieties after flowering in spring. Species can be grown from seed sown fresh.
Hesperis (Sweet rocket)	Seed sown in spring is the normal means of increase, but the double-flowered type does not set seed and basal cuttings must be taken in spring, preferably after cutting back to induce new growth of suitable material.
Heuchera	Division of named varieties in spring, summer or autumn. Some, with careful selection of seedlings, come true from seed. Species are grown from seed sown in spring.

PLANT	PROPAGATION METHODS
Hibiscus (Mallow)	The annuals, perennials and shrubs can all be grown from seed, which needs chipping and/or soaking overnight. Perennials can be divided in spring or ripe cuttings taken in autumn. Shrubby ones are best layered.
Hoheria	Softwood cuttings in summer or layering.
Hosta	Division of the congested roots in spring is not easy but is the best method of increase (*see* page 57); each piece must have a bud on it. Species can be grown from seed sown fresh or in spring, but take several years to reach flowering size.
Humulus (Hop)	Division of crowns in spring.
Hyacinthoides (Bluebell)	These can multiply all too readily by self-sowing. They can be divided, but bulbs are often deep down. Sow seed fresh and divide after flowering, preferably when plants are dormant.
Hyacinthus (Hyacinth)	Division of offsets that form around the main bulb after flowering in spring. Also, by scooping and scoring.
Hydrangea	Softwood cuttings in spring or semi-ripe cuttings in summer.
Hypericum (St John's wort)	Division in spring of spreading herbaceous and shrubby plants such as *H. calycinum*. Softwood, greenwood or semi-ripe cuttings, with a heel, in summer for most of the shrubby forms. Sow seed of species fresh or in spring.
Hyssopus (Hyssop)	Can be increased from seed, division or cuttings in spring. Cuttings can also be taken in summer and autumn.
Iberis (Candytuft)	Semi-ripe cuttings in summer. Can also be increased by division after flowering or from seed in spring or autumn.
Ilex (Holly)	Semi-ripe cuttings in summer or autumn. Non-named varieties can be grown from seed, preferably after chilling.
Impatiens (Busy lizzie)	Most come readily from cuttings taken any time of the year. Pre-chill seed and sow in gentle heat in spring, but do not cover with compost as the seed needs light.
Incarvillea (Trumpet flower)	Generally increased from seed, preferably sown fresh, but it takes several years to reach flowering size. Some types can be carefully divided.
Indigofera	Softwood cuttings in spring or summer.
Inula	Clump-forming perennials that can be easily divided in spring or autumn. Species can be grown from seed sown fresh or in spring; do not cover seed too deeply, as some light is beneficial to germination.
Ipheion	These bulbs multiply quite quickly and are easy to divide once flowering is over.
Ipomoea	Sow seed in gentle heat and take tip cuttings in spring.
Iris	Most types can be divided, usually after flowering. Those with thick rhizomes can be cut into sections, each with a bud. All non-named varieties will propagate by seed, preferably sown fresh.
Itea (Sweet spire)	Semi-ripe cuttings in summer.
Jasminum (Jasmine)	Semi-ripe cuttings in summer or layering.

PLANT	PROPAGATION METHODS
Jasione	Usually grown from seed sown fresh or in spring. Some can be divided.
Jeffersonia	Sow seed when fresh or divide carefully in spring.
Juncus (Rush)	Best divided in spring. Will also propagate from fresh seed sown in compost which is kept wet.
Kalanchoe	Sow seed in gentle heat in spring to autumn. Leaf cuttings from spring to summer or stem cuttings from spring to autumn.
Kalmia	Easy to layer. Semi-ripe cuttings in summer are trickier. Also propagates by seed sown fresh or in spring. Seed is poisonous.
Kerria (Jew's mantle)	Division of suckering rootstocks in autumn or spring. Hardwood cuttings in winter.
Kirengeshoma	Division in spring.
Kolkwitzia	Softwood cuttings in spring, greenwood and semi-ripe cuttings in summer.
Knautia	Division in spring or autumn. Seed preferably sown fresh, but can also be sown in spring.
Kniphofia (Red-hot poker)	Can be divided at any time of year when the plant is in active growth, but usually in spring. Divisions separate easily under water.
Lamium (Dead nettle)	Division in spring or autumn is the easiest method. Species such as *L. orvala* come easily from seed sown fresh or in spring. Basal cuttings in spring.
Lathyrus (Everlasting pea, sweet pea)	Seed is the easiest method of increase. Scarify or soak the seed overnight before sowing. Some spreading forms, such as *L. grandiflorus*, can be divided in spring.
Laurus (Bay)	Semi-ripe cuttings in summer.
Lavandula (Lavender)	Softwood, greenwood or semi-ripe cuttings in spring or summer.
Lavatera (Mallow)	Tip cuttings in spring, summer or autumn. A few multi-stemmed types can be divided in spring. Annuals come easily from seed, as do species such as *L. cachemiriana*.
Leucojum (Snowflake)	Like most bulbs, these can be divided easily after flowering.
Lewisia	Grown mainly from seed sown fresh. Some species make offsets and these can be divided in summer.
Liatris (Blazing star, gay feather)	Division in spring or autumn, cutting with a knife. Species come easily from seed sown in spring or autumn.
Libertia	Division in spring or autumn. They will also propagate by seed sown in spring.
Ligularia	Usually division in spring or autumn, but species can be grown from seed sown in spring.
Ligustrum (Privet)	Semi-ripe cuttings in summer or hardwood cuttings in winter.
Lilium (Lily)	Lilies are not difficult to propagate, but there are a lot of different methods and anyone becoming keen should consult specialist books, especially for growing from seed and techniques of scaling. For many, seed can be sown fresh, but dormancy

PLANT	PROPAGATION METHODS
Lilium (continued)	may need to be broken by chilling. It takes several years to get a flowering plant from seed. Scaling is a possibility for many types (*see* page 62). Those that produce bulbils can be increased by sowing these fresh (*see* page 60). Stoloniferous or rhizomatous plants can be divided in autumn.
Limonium (Sea lavender, statice)	Division in spring. Some, especially *L. latifolium*, can be increased from root cuttings in winter. Annuals and species can be grown from seed sown in spring.
Linaria (Toadflax)	Self-propagating from seed or vigorously spreading by underground stems. If the self-sown seedlings are not enough, seed can be sown or plants be divided in spring or autumn.
Linum (Flax)	Seed sown in spring. Will also self-sow. Named varieties can be grown from tip cuttings in spring.
Liriope	Easily divided in spring.
Lobelia	Annuals and species propagate easily from seed sown in spring. Division is also easy for many. Stem cuttings can be taken in summer or after flowering.
Lonicera (Honeysuckle)	Both the climbers and the shrubs will root from semi-ripe cuttings in summer. They can also be increased by hardwood cuttings in winter.
Lunaria (Honesty)	They all come easily from seed and the perennial, *L. rediviva*, can be divided in spring.
Lupinus (Lupin)	These come readily from seed. It helps to scarify, chip or soak the seed before sowing. Most can also be increased from basal cuttings taken in spring.
Lychnis (Catchfly)	Seed sown in spring is the usual method of increase. Some, such as the colourful *L. × haageana*, need to be propagated by division in spring or autumn.
Lysimachia (Loosestrife)	Most are easily increased by division in spring or autumn.
Lythrum (Purple loosestrife)	Division in spring or autumn, but they will also come from basal cuttings in spring.
Magnolia	Softwood cuttings in spring for some, greenwood or semi-ripe cuttings in summer or autumn for most. Layering in spring if the branches low enough; alternatively, air layering is a possibility. Many varieties are grafted.
Macleaya (Plume poppy)	Division in spring. Root cuttings can be taken in winter.
Mahonia (Oregon grape)	Semi-ripe or leaf-bud cuttings in summer, but they can be slow to root.
Malus (Crab apple)	Can only be propagated by grafting, including budding.
Malva (Mallow)	Seed sown in spring provides the best way of increase. Cuttings from sideshoots or tip cuttings can also be taken in spring or summer.
Matteuccia (Ostrich fern)	Division is easy in spring or sow ripe spores.
Matthiola (Stock)	The annuals and biennials are grown from seed sown fresh or in spring. Some perennial forms can be increased by division in spring.
Meconopsis	Most can be propagated from seed, which must be sown fresh. Do not cover the seed with compost, as it needs light, and keep it moist. Perennial forms can be divided in spring.

PLANT	PROPAGATION METHODS
Melianthus (Honey bush)	Perennials are sometimes treated as annuals and grown from seed sown in spring. Rooted suckers can be removed from established plants in spring, and cuttings taken at the same time.
Melica (Melick)	Grasses that are divided in spring or grown from seed sown in spring.
Melissa (Balm)	Usually sown from seed, although they self-sow prolifically, producing enough seedlings for most purposes.
Milium (Millet)	Grasses that can be divided in spring or grown from seed sown in autumn or spring.
Mimulus (Monkey flower)	Seed sown in spring or in autumn under glass. Division or tip cuttings in spring.
Miscanthus	A large genus of grasses that can be divided in spring. Old established clumps will need some effort.
Monarda (Bergamot)	Spreading clumps can be easily divided in spring or autumn. Basal cuttings can also be taken in spring.
Moraea	Division in autumn. Seed sown in autumn or spring.
Muscari (Grape hyacinth)	As with most bulbs, these are easy to divide in autumn. They also come very easily from seed sown in autumn and self-sow copiously.
Myosotis (Forget-me-not)	Seed sown in autumn or spring is the easiest method both for annuals and perennials. The former self-sow prodigiously. Perennials can also be divided in spring or autumn.
Myrrhis (Sweet cicely)	Grows easily from seed sown fresh or in spring.
Myrtus	Semi-ripe cuttings taken in summer.
Narcissus (Daffodil)	Division when they are dormant is the most common method, although species can be grown from freshly sown seed.
Nectaroscordum	Come very readily from seed and can self-sow prolifically. They can be divided but the bulbs are usually very deep in the soil.
Nemophila	Sow seed in spring. Self-sow freely.
Nepeta (Catmint)	These come easily from division in spring. Alternatively, by basal or tip cuttings, also in spring.
Nerine	Bulbs are easy to divide after flowering.
Nerium (Oleander)	Softwood cuttings in spring.
Nicotiana (Tobacco plant)	Seed sown in gentle heat in spring is the usual way of propagating both annuals and perennials.
Nigella (Love-in-a-mist)	Annuals that propagate easily from seed sown in autumn or in spring. They will self-sow, producing plenty of seedlings.
Nuphar (Yellow pond lily)	Divide in spring and plant back in the pond or in compost in containers placed under water.

PLANT	PROPAGATION METHODS
Nymphaea (Water lily)	Divide in spring; keep divisions wet. Alternatively, sow fresh seed in wet compost.
Oenothera (Evening primrose)	Main method of increase is seed sown in spring. Some have very hard seedpods and need to be soaked in water to release the seed. Some perennials can be increased from basal or stem cuttings in spring or summer or divided in spring.
Olearia (Daisy bush)	Softwood, greenwood or semi-ripe cuttings in summer.
Omphalodes (Navelwort)	Annuals and many perennials can be grown from seed sown in autumn or spring. Other perennials can be divided, preferably in autumn but also spring.
Onoclea (Sensitive fern)	Division in spring or spores sown ripe.
Onopordum (Scotch thistle)	Seed is the only method of increase of these biennials. Sow either fresh or in spring. They will self-sow.
Onosma	Seed sown in spring is the main method, although tip cuttings taken in spring are an alternative.
Ophiopogon (Lilyturf)	Easily increased by division in autumn or spring. Non-named varieties can also be grown from spring-sown seed.
Ornithogalum (Star-of-Bethlehem)	These produce plenty of offsets and are easily divided after flowering.
Osmanthus	Semi-ripe cuttings in summer.
Osmunda (Royal fern)	Division in spring or sow ripe spores.
Osteospermum	Increase from tip cuttings at any time during the growing season. Can also be grown from seed sown in gentle heat in spring.
Oxalis (Shamrock, sorrel)	The bulbous forms can usually be multiplied by dividing offsets. Some can be increased by dividing the rhizomes. Most, except named varieties, can be grown from freshly sown seed.
Paeonia (Peony)	The usual way of increase of herbaceous peonies is by careful division in autumn or spring, ensuring that each piece has at least one eye. Species can be grown from freshly sown seed; dried-out seed is likely to take several years to germinate, if it ever does (pre-chilling might help dried-out seed). Tree peonies can be propagated by semi-ripe cuttings in summer; named varieties need to be wedge-grafted in summer.
Papaver (Poppy)	Seed is the best way for annuals and species. Many self-sow. Named varieties of perennials, such as those of *P. orientalis,* can be grown from root cuttings taken in winter. Division is not easy but can be done in spring.
Paradisea (Paradise lily)	Can easily be divided, preferably in autumn but also in spring. Alternatively, sow seed in autumn or spring.
Paris	These rhizomatous woodlanders can be divided in autumn once the foliage has died down. Also, they can be grown from seed sown in autumn, although the plants can take several years to reach flowering size.

PLANT	PROPAGATION METHODS
Passiflora (Passionflower)	Softwood, greenwood or semi-ripe cuttings from spring to summer. Sow seeds and layer at any time.
Pelargonium	Tip cuttings at any time, but preferably in autumn and overwinter under glass. After taking cuttings, leave them in the open air for a couple of days to callus and then put into the cutting mixture.
Pennisetum	Divide in spring. Both annuals and perennials can also be grown from seed sown in spring.
Penstemon	Tip or stem cuttings in spring and summer.
Perovskia	Basal cuttings in spring is the best and easiest method.
Persicaria	Division in autumn or spring is easy for most plants. Seed sown in spring is another possibility.
Petasites (Butterbur)	These invasive plants can be divided easily, preferably after flowering, but timing doesn't really matter.
Petunia	Short-lived perennials that are treated as annuals. Sow seed in gentle heat in spring.
Phalaris (Canary grass, gardener's garters)	Division in spring is easy. Annuals are grown from seed sown in spring.
Philadelphus (Mock orange)	Softwood, greenwood or semi-ripe cuttings in summer. Hardwood cuttings in autumn or winter.
Phlomis	Perennial types and shrubby ones that spread (for instance *P. italicum*) can be divided easily in autumn or spring. The shrubbier members can be increased from softwood, greenwood or semi-ripe cuttings taken in spring, summer or autumn.
Phlox	Healthy tall border phloxes can be divided in spring or basal cuttings can be taken at the same time of year, but if they are suffering from eel worm, root cuttings taken in winter are safer. The low-growing, mat-forming types can be increased from tip cuttings taken after flowering in summer. The dwarf species, such as *P. divaricata*, can be divided or tip cuttings taken in spring.
Phormium	Divide in spring, although this may be difficult with larger plants. Some sideshoots, when removed, may not have any roots, but these will quickly grow.
Photinia	Semi-ripe cuttings in summer.
Phuopsis	Easy to divide in spring.
Phygelius (Cape figwort)	Softwood cuttings in summer. Division is also possible for clump-forming types.
Phyllostachys (Golden bamboo)	Division in spring as it comes into growth.
Physalis (Chinese lantern)	Rhizomatous growth can be divided easily in spring.

PLANT	PROPAGATION METHODS
Physostegia (Obedient plant)	Easy to divide in spring. Alternatively, basal cuttings can also be taken in spring.
Pieris	Can be increased by layering or semi-ripe cuttings taken in summer.
Pittosporum	Semi-ripe cuttings in summer. Species can be grown from fresh seed, first removing the flesh.
Plantago	Garden-worthy forms can be divided in spring.
Platycodon (Balloon flower)	Division, basal cuttings or seed sown in spring.
Plumbago (Leadwort)	Annuals grown from seed in spring. Others can be divided in spring or take semi-ripe cuttings in summer.
Poa (Meadow grass)	Annuals sown from seed in spring. Perennials can also be propagated by seed but they can also be divided in spring.
Polemonium (Jacob's ladder)	Clump-forming species can be divided in spring or autumn. They can also be sown from seed, either fresh or in spring.
Polygonatum (Solomon's seal)	Their creeping tendency means they can be divided easily, preferably in autumn, but also in spring after flowering.
Polypodium (Polypody fern)	Divide in spring. Ripe spores can also be sown. Some species produce bulbils, which can be rooted by pegging the frond down on moist compost.
Polystichum (Shield fern)	Divide rhizomes in spring or sow ripe spores. Some species also produce bulbils, which can be rooted by pegging the frond down on moist compost.
Potentilla (Cinquefoil)	Semi-ripe cuttings of shrubby types in summer. Herbaceous forms can be increased by division in spring or autumn, while some can be layered from runners. Annuals should be grown from seed sown in spring.
Primula (Primrose)	Most can be increased by division after flowering. Seed is also an option, but must be sown fresh, mixed with sand and not covered with compost.
Prunus (Ornamental cherry)	Softwood cuttings in spring or semi-ripe cuttings in summer. Those that are difficult are best increased by grafting. Those with suckering rootstocks, such as varieties of *P. tenella*, can be divided.
Pulmonaria (Lungwort)	Division is easy and should be carried out after flowering. Root cuttings in autumn. They do self-sow, but seedlings do not necessarily come true except for species.
Pulsatilla	Propagates easily from seed sown in spring to summer. Division is sometimes suggested as an option, but it is not easy. Root cuttings taken in winter are the only way of obtaining named varieties.
Puschkinia	Lift and divide the offsets when the bulbs are dormant. They can also be sown from fresh seed.
Pyracantha (Firethorn)	Semi-ripe cuttings in summer. Can also be layered.
Pyrus (Ornamental pear)	Graft onto a pear or quince rootstock.
Quercus (Oak)	Seed (acorns) sown fresh or grafting onto an oak rootstock. Some evergreen varieties will also propagate by softwood cuttings taken in spring.

PLANT	PROPAGATION METHODS
Ranunculus (Buttercup)	Apart from named varieties, most grow easily from seed, as long as it is sown fresh. Division in spring is usually possible with most forms. *R. ficaria* produces bulbils in its axils which can be sown fresh.
Rhodiola	Clump-forming types can be divided easily in autumn or spring. Most will also come from leaf cuttings. Tip or stem cuttings can be taken in spring.
Rhododendron (Azalea, rhododendron)	Semi-ripe cuttings in summer is the easiest method, although some of the larger-flowered hybrids need to be grafted. Many can be layered, often self-layering in the surrounding soil.
Ribes (Flowering currant)	Semi-ripe cuttings in summer or hardwood cuttings in autumn.
Ricinus	Shrub but usually treated as an annual. Grow from seed sown in gentle heat in spring. Seed is very poisonous.
Robinia	Named varieties can be grafted onto seed-grown rootstock of *R. pseudoacacia*, but others will come from seed sown fresh.
Rodgersia	Division in autumn or spring.
Romneya (Tree poppy)	The best way is to take root cuttings in winter. There is a better success rate with horizontally laid cuttings. They can be divided, but with difficulty, as soil usually falls off and it is difficult to find rooted sections.
Rosa (Rose)	Budding is the most common commercial method, but for the amateur semi-ripe cuttings in spring or summer, or hardwood cuttings in winter, are good methods. Layer roses with lax, spreading branches, such as ramblers and ground-cover roses. Species can be increased from freshly sown seed. (*See also* box, page 65.)
Roscoea	Divide tubers in spring or grow from fresh-sown seed.
Rubus (Flowering bramble)	Semi-ripe cuttings in summer. They are often clump-forming, so can be divided in autumn or spring. Many root at the tips, providing layers.
Rudbeckia (Coneflower)	Annuals are sown from seed. Others can be divided easily in autumn after flowering or in spring. It is also often possible to pull off pieces of rooted cuttings at any time of year.
Ruta (Rue)	Easily comes from cuttings, especially those taken in summer. Some people are allergic to rue, so avoid skin contact.
Saintpaulia (African violet)	The easiest way is by leaf cuttings when plants are in growth. Can also be divided in spring. Seeds can be sown in gentle heat in spring.
Salix (Willow)	Softwood, greenwood or semi-ripe cuttings in summer. Hardwood cuttings in autumn. Sow fresh seed in spring or summer. Can also be propagated by grafting.
Salvia (Sage)	Can be increased by cuttings taken in spring. The annuals and those perennials treated as annuals should be grown from seed sown in spring. Some, such as *S. patens*, can be divided. (For culinary sage, *see* page 91.)
Sambucus (Elder)	Most are shrubby plants that can all be increased from semi-ripe cuttings in summer or hardwood cuttings in winter. Special varieties can be grafted or grown from layers. The one herbaceous species, *S. ebulus*, can be divided or grown from seed sown in spring or autumn.

PLANT	PROPAGATION METHODS
Sanguinaria (Bloodroot)	Divide the spreading rhizomes when the plants are dormant. The single-flowered species can also be sown from fresh seed.
Sanguisorba (Burnet)	Division in autumn or spring is the easiest method, especially with those that spread extensively. They can also be grown from spring-sown seed. Will self-sow.
Sansevieria	Division in spring. Leaf cuttings during the growing season.
Santolina (Cotton lavender)	Softwood, greenwood or semi-ripe cuttings any time in the growing season.
Saponaria (Soapwort)	Take tip cuttings or sow seed, both in spring. Those that spread, such as the vigorous *S. officinalis*, can be divided easily in autumn or spring.
Sarcococca (Christmas box)	Easily divided in spring or autumn. Semi-ripe cuttings in summer; hardwood cuttings in autumn.
Sasa (Dwarf bamboo)	Division in spring as growth starts.
Satureja (Savory)	Most can be increased from seed sown in spring. Perennial forms can be increased from spring cuttings.
Schizanthus (Poor man's orchid)	Sow seed in gentle heat in spring.
Scutellaria (Skullcap)	Division or basal cuttings, both in spring. Seed can be sown in spring. Some self-sow.
Sedum	Clump-forming types can be divided easily in autumn or spring. Most will also come from leaf cuttings. Tip or stem cuttings can also be taken in spring.
Sempervivum (House leek)	Detach the offsets and plant in cutting compost at any time throughout the growing season.
Senecio	A very large genus with some weeds but also plenty of good plants, which can be divided in spring or autumn. Alternatively, tip cuttings can be taken in spring. Seed can be sown in spring; some need light so should not be covered.
Serratula (Sawwort)	Division in autumn after flowering or, better still, in spring.
Shortia	Careful division in spring. Seed is difficult but should be sown fresh and a period of chilling may be beneficial.
Sidalcea (Prairie mallow)	Division in spring or autumn is the best method. Species can be sown from fresh seed.
Silene (Campion)	Propagate readily from the copious amounts of seed they produce. Sow fresh or in spring. Most can also be divided, preferably in autumn for spring-flowering varieties.
Silybum	From seed sown in spring or autumn. Will self-sow.
Sisyrinchium	Division is very easy more or less at any time of year, although spring is probably best. Also come easily, perhaps too easily, from seed. Some self-sow vigorously.
Skimmia	Suckers can be removed in spring or autumn. Semi-ripe cuttings can be taken in summer or autumn.

PLANT	PROPAGATION METHODS
Smyrnium	Biennials that come easily from seed. Best sown directly where they are to flower. Will self-sow once established.
Solenostemon (Coleus)	Seed from spring to summer. Tip cuttings from named cultivars.
Solidago (Golden rod)	Clump-formers that can easily be divided in spring or autumn.
Sorbus (Rowan)	Species can be grown from seed sown fresh, named varieties from grafting.
Sphaeralcea (Globe mallow)	Although not readily set in cultivation, seed is the main way of propagation. Young tip cuttings taken in spring is another method.
Spartium (Spanish broom)	Semi-ripe cuttings in summer.
Spiraea	Semi-ripe cuttings in summer. Some will come from hardwood cuttings in winter.
Stachys (Betony, woundwort)	Most are creeping or clump-forming and can be easily divided in spring or autumn. Species can be grown from seed sown in spring.
Sternbergia (Autumn daffodil)	Division of these bulbous plants in spring just before foliage dies down, or in autumn while the plants are still dormant. Fresh-sown seed is another possibility, but takes some years before flowering.
Stipa (Feather grass)	Division in spring just as growth begins. Species can also be grown from spring-sown seed.
Stokesia (Stokes' aster)	Division is easy in spring. An alternative is root cuttings taken in winter. Will also come from seed sown fresh or in spring.
Stylophorum	Woodlanders that can be increased from seed, preferably sown fresh but also in spring. With care they can also be divided in either spring or autumn.
Styrax	From layers taken in spring or seed sown fresh or in spring. Also from semi-ripe cuttings in summer.
Symphytum (Comfrey)	Very easy to propagate by dividing the rapidly spreading plants in spring or autumn. Although hardly necessary, they will also come readily from root cuttings taken in winter.
Syringa (Lilac)	Species will come from seed sown fresh or in spring. Named cultivars are grafted.
Tagetes (Marigold)	From seed sown in gentle heat in spring.
Tamarix (Tamarisk)	Softwood cuttings in spring or summer or hardwood cuttings in winter. Seed can be sown in spring.
Tanacetum	These spreading plants are easy to divide in spring or autumn.
Tellima (Fringecups)	This plant self-sows and rarely needs propagating, but it can be increased from seed sown fresh or in spring, or by division in spring.
Teucrium	These can either be divided or cuttings taken, both in spring. Seed can be sown fresh or in spring.
Thalictrum (Meadow rue)	Division in spring, although divisions can be slow to re-establish and may take a while to flower. Sow seed fresh or in spring.

PLANT	PROPAGATION METHODS
Thermopsis	Sow seed in spring, soaking the hard seed overnight beforehand. Also, by division or basal cuttings in spring.
Tiarella (Foamflower)	Creeping habit makes it easy to divide in spring or autumn.
Tithonia (Mexican sunflower)	Seed sown in gentle heat in spring.
Tolmiea (Pick-aback plant, piggy-back plant)	Produces plantlets on its leaf-stalks that can be rooted. The plants themselves can also be divided.
Tradescantia (Spiderwort)	Division in spring or autumn is the easiest method of increase. Border plants will also self-sow.
Tricyrtis (Toad lily)	Easy to divide the rhizomes in spring, before growth starts. Can also be grown from freshly sown seed.
Trifolium (Clover)	Seed sown in spring is one of the easiest methods. Division in spring is also a possibility, in spite of the fact that some have tap roots.
Trillium (Wake robin, wood lily)	Not easily to propagate. Division immediately after flowering is one method. Also, from seed sown fresh, but the resulting plants take several years to reach flowering size. Pre-chilling the seed helps break dormancy.
Trollius (Globeflower)	Division after flowering in spring or in autumn. Seed must be sown fresh.
Tropaeolum (Nasturtium)	Seed sown in spring is the normal method. Perennials can also be increased by division of their tubers in spring, although these are often very deep in the soil. A few can be increased from basal cuttings in spring.
Tulbaghia	Easily lifted and divided after flowering. Will also come from seed sown fresh or in spring.
Tulipa (Tulip)	Easily divided during their dormant period. Species can also be grown from freshly sown seed.
Uvularia (Merrybells)	Creeping woodlanders that can easily be divided in autumn or spring, after flowering. Seed can be sown fresh or in spring.
Vaccinium (Blueberry, whortleberry)	Decorative ground-cover plants that can be divided easily in spring or autumn. They also layer very easily and will come from fresh- or spring-sown seed.
Valeriana	Seed sown in spring is a good option, but should not be sown too deeply as it likes some light. Basal cuttings can be attempted in spring, or they can be divided in spring or autumn.
Veratrum	These are monocarpic and die after flowering, but often produce offsets which can be lifted, replanted and grown on. Seed can be sown fresh, but the resulting bulbs can take up to eight years before reaching flowering size – and then they die!
Verbascum (Mullein)	The biennial verbascums are all grown from seed, sown either fresh or in spring. There are usually copious self-sown seedlings. The perennial types also propagate from seed, but special forms can often be increased by dividing secondary rosettes in spring if any have been formed, or by taking root cuttings in winter.

PLANT	PROPAGATION METHODS
Verbena	Annuals and tender perennials treated as annuals can often be grown from seed sown in spring. Some need light and gentle heat to germinate. Some species, such as *V. bonariensis*, self-sow prolifically. They can also be increased from basal cuttings from plants overwintered in frost-free conditions or tip cuttings, both in spring.
Vernonia (Ironweed)	Most of this large genus are spreaders and can be divided easily in spring. Basal cuttings can be taken in spring or seed sown in spring.
Veronica (Speedwell)	Most come readily from division in spring or autumn. They will also come from seed, but do not cover too deeply as they like some light to germinate. Can also be propagated by tip cuttings in spring.
Veronicastrum (Culver's root)	Related to *Veronica* and propagated in the same way.
Viburnum	Softwood, greenwood or semi-ripe cuttings in summer. Species can be grown from their berries sown fresh or in spring (remove flesh before sowing).
Vinca (Periwinkle)	Shrubby plants that root easily where their tips touch the ground. These can be treated as divisions or layers. Tip cuttings can also be taken in summer.
Viola (Pansy, violet)	Species and bedding forms can be grown from seed sown in spring or autumn. Special forms (including any bedding plants you would like to perpetuate) can be increased from basal cuttings or tip cuttings in spring or other times of year by shearing over the plant and getting new growth. Division from spring to autumn.
Waldsteinia	Rhizomatous woodland plants that can be divided easily in spring or autumn. They can also be grown from spring-sown seed.
Weigela	Softwood, greenwood or semi-ripe cuttings taken in summer, or from hardwood cuttings taken in autumn or winter.
Woodwardia (Chain fern)	Division as plants come into growth in spring or from ripe spores. Some species produce bulbils, which can be rooted by pegging the frond down on moist compost.
Wulfenia	Divide the rhizomatous plants in spring or autumn. They will also propagate by seed sown in spring.
Yucca	Seed needs to be propagated at between 20 and 30°C (68 and 86°F). Yuccas can also be grown from root cuttings taken in winter, if you can bear to dig up the plants. Suckering species can be propagated by dividing from sideshoots in autumn.
Zantedeschia (Arum lily)	Divide in spring while the plants are still dormant. Root cuttings can be taken in winter and non-named varieties can be increased from seed sown in spring; keep the compost moist.
Zauschneria (Californian fuchsia)	From tip cuttings spring or summer. With care, they can also be divided in spring. Sow seed in gentle heat in spring.
Zephyranthes	Bulbs that can easily be divided when dormant.
Zinnia	Sow seed in gentle heat in spring. Can be sown outside when the weather is warmer.

Fruit, vegetables and common herbs

PLANT	PROPAGATION METHODS
Apples	Pips will produce trees but rarely the same as the parent. Grafting is the most usual way of propagation. However, you have to be careful of the rootstock used, as this will affect the size and vigour of the tree. Here are some of the rootstocks available: M27 very dwarf 1.8 m 6ft) MM106 semi-vigorous 4.5m (15ft) M9 dwarf 2.4m (8ft) MM111 vigorous 5.5m (18ft) M26 semi-dwarf 3m (10ft)
Apricots	Avoid growing from stones, as they are not likely to come true. Graft onto special rootstock in winter. St Julien A is vigorous and suitable for bushes or training into fan shapes; Brompton A is vigorous and suitable for bushes.
Artichokes, globe	Divide plants in spring and plant offsets at 75–90cm (30–36in) intervals. Can be grown from seed sown under glass or in open ground in spring.
Artichokes, Jerusalem	Plant tubers 15cm (6in) deep at 30cm (12in) intervals. Large tubers can be cut into sections as long as each has at least one eye.
Asparagus	Divide existing plants in autumn once they are dormant. Can be grown from fresh seed sown in pots or in open ground.
Aubergines	Sow seed under cover in gentle heat in spring, and except in warm areas grow the plants in the greenhouse. In warmer areas, plant out at 60cm (24in) intervals.
Basil	Sow seed under cover in gentle heat in spring or outdoors in summer.
Beetroot	Sow seed where they are to grow. Sow spring to summer to get successional crops. Station sow at 7.5–10cm (3–4in).
Blackberries	Long branches usually arc down and layer where the tips touch the soil. You can dig up these layers or deliberately form your own layers using the tip-layering technique (*see* page 54).
Blackcurrants	Come readily from hardwood cuttings taken in autumn or winter.
Blueberries	Take softwood, greenwood or semi-ripe cuttings in spring or summer.
Broad beans	Usually sow where they are to grow in early winter or early spring. Sow seed at 20–23cm (8–9in) intervals. Can be sown in pots or modules under glass and planted out when big enough.
Broccoli, sprouting	Can be sown in spring in a seed bed in the open ground, or in trays or pots under cover in spring. Plant out at 45–60cm (18–24in) intervals.
Brussels sprouts	Sow either outside in a seed bed or in trays or pots under cover in spring. Transplant to 50–75cm (20–30in) intervals.
Cabbages	Can be sown in pots or trays inside but more usually in a seed bed in the open garden in spring, summer or autumn, depending on variety. Transplant to 50–75cm (20–30in) intervals.
Calabrese (Green broccoli)	Can be sown in pots or modules, but best sown where they are to grow in spring, as they resent disturbance. Sow or transplant at 30–45cm (12–18in) intervals.
Carrots	Sow thinly in rows where they are to grow. Sow from early spring though to summer for a succession of crops.

PLANT	PROPAGATION METHODS
Cauliflowers	Sow in a seed bed in spring or in pots or trays at the same time of year. Transplant to 50–75cm (20–30in) intervals.
Celeriac	Sow in trays or modules under glass in spring. Plant out after frosts have passed at 30cm (12in) intervals.
Celery	Sow in trays or modules under glass in spring. Plant out after frosts have passed at 23cm (9in) intervals.
Cherries	Seed is not a real possibility. Grafting in winter is the usual way, usually these days on a dwarfing stock such as Colt, Gisela 5 or Gisela 6.
Chicory	Sow in spring or summer in open ground. Thin to 25–30cm (10–12in) intervals.
Chillies	Sow in pots or trays under glass in gentle heat in spring, transplant into pots and keep under glass or polytunnels.
Chives	Divide clumps in spring or autumn or sow seed under cover in spring.
Courgettes	Sow in individual pots or modules in gentle heat in spring and move outside once frosts have finished. Plant out at 60cm (24in) intervals. Can be station sown where they are to grow in spring or summer.
Cucumbers	Sow in individual pots or modules in gentle heat in spring and transfer to large pots or growing bags within the greenhouse. Outside varieties can be moved outside after the frosts.
Damsons	Can be grown from stones. For the home-grower, division is often the easiest answer. They often produce suckers, which can be divided off in autumn or spring.
Endive	Sow in a seed bed in spring or summer and transplant to 25–30cm (10–12in) intervals.
Florence fennel	Sow directly where they are to grow in summer. Station sow at 30cm (12in) intervals.
Figs	Take hardwood cuttings in autumn or winter. Layer in spring or summer, although layers can be slow to take.
French beans	Sow in shallow trenches in spring to summer. Sow or thin to 10cm (4in) intervals. They can be sown in pots or modules under cover and transplanted in spring, when frosts have passed.
Garlic	Plant individual cloves directly into the soil in autumn, winter or early spring at 15cm (6in) intervals.
Gooseberries	Take hardwood cuttings in autumn or winter.
Grapes	Take hardwood cuttings in autumn or winter.
Kale	Sow in a seed bed in spring or summer and transplant to 45–60cm (18–24in) intervals.
Kohl rabi	Sow in rows in spring directly where they are to grow, thinning when seedlings are big enough to 15–20cm (6–8in) intervals.
Leeks	Sow in spring in seed beds or in pots, trays or modules under cover. Transplant to 15cm (6in) intervals.

PLANT	PROPAGATION METHODS
Lettuces	Sow in a seed bed from spring onwards for a succession. Can also be sown under glass in pots, trays or modules. Plant out at 23–30cm (9–12in) intervals. Summer sowings should be sown where they are to grow and thinned, not transplanted, as the latter tends to bolt.
Loganberries	Long branches usually arc down and layer where the tips touch in summer or autumn. You can dig up these layers or deliberately form tip layers (*see* page 54).
Marjoram/oregano	Grow from seed sown fresh or in spring. They self-sow. Most can also be divided in spring.
Marrows	Sow in individual pots or modules in gentle heat in spring and move outside once frosts have finished. Plant out at 60–90cm (24–36in) intervals. Can be station sown where they are to grow in summer.
Melons	Sow seed in spring under glass in gentle heat.
Mint	These herbs run underground and are easily divided in autumn or spring. Invasive.
Mulberries	Branches are often low enough to layer. Taking hardwood cuttings in autumn or winter is also a good method. Species can be grown from seed, but this is slow.
Nectarines	Grow either from seed sown fresh after a period of chilling or from hardwood cuttings in winter. Most varieties are grafted in winter.
Onions	Usually planted as 'sets' (small bulbs) in spring at 10cm (4in) intervals. Can also be sown under glass in winter, potted on and planted out when big enough in spring.
Parsley	Sow seed under glass in gentle heat in spring or outdoors when the soil has warmed up.
Parsnips	Station sow at 15–20cm (6–8in) in rows where they are to grow in spring.
Peaches	Take hardwood cuttings in winter or sow fresh seed after a period of chilling, although they are not likely to come true. Most varieties are grafted in winter.
Pears	Graft in winter onto a quince rootstock. Quince A is a dwarfing stock while Quince C is a more vigorous one. For standard trees, pear rootstock is used.
Peas	Usually sown in a shallow trench at 5cm (2in) intervals from spring to summer for succession, but can also be grown in pots and carefully transplanted.
Peppers	Sow in pots or modules under glass in gentle heat in spring and continue to grow under glass or in polytunnels except in warm areas.
Plums	Can be grown from seed, but results are unpredictable. Grafting in winter is the usual method. Pixie rootstock is relatively dwarfing, while Julien A is vigorous.
Potatoes	Plant 'seed' potatoes where they are to grow from early spring onwards. Plant in trenches 13–15cm (5–6in) deep at 30–35cm (12–15in) apart. Large potatoes can be cut into sections, as long as each has an eye on it.
Pumpkins	Sow in individual pots or modules in spring and move outside once frosts have finished. Plant out at 90cm (36in) intervals. Can be station sown where they are to grow when the soil has warmed up.
Quinces	Suitable rootstocks for grafting are Quince A, a dwarfing stock, and Quince C, a more vigorous one. Can also be propagated from hardwood cuttings in autumn.

PLANT	PROPAGATION METHODS
Radishes	Sow where they are to grow from spring onwards for successional crops, thinning to 2.5–5cm (1–2in) apart.
Raspberries	These produce plenty of suckers which can easily be divided in autumn or spring.
Redcurrants	Take hardwood cuttings in autumn or winter.
Rhubarb	Divide crowns in winter or spring and replant at 75–90cm (30–36in) intervals.
Rosemary	Take semi-ripe cuttings with a heel in summer.
Runner beans	Sow one or two beans at 23–30cm (9–12in) intervals where they are to grow in spring and thin if necessary. Can also be sown in individual pots or modules under cover and transplanted.
Sage	Take tip cuttings in spring. Layer after flowering. Sow seed of species in spring.
Salsify	Sow where it is to grow in spring and thin to 15cm (6in).
Sea kale	Carefully divide and replant crowns in spring at 38cm (15in) intervals.
Shallots	Plant bulbs at 15cm (6in) intervals in open ground where they are to grow in winter.
Spinach	Sow where it is to grow from spring onwards for succession. Thin to 15cm (6in).
Spinach, perpetual	Sow in spring or summer. Thin to 15cm (6in).
Spring onions	Sow seed where it is to grow from spring onwards for succession. Thin to 2.5cm (1in).
Squashes	Sow in individual pots or modules in gentle heat in spring and move outside once frosts have finished. Plant out at 90cm (3ft) intervals. Can be station sown where they are to grow when the soil has warmed up.
Strawberries	These send out runners in summer and autumn, which root as they spread. These can easily be lifted and used as new plants or pinned into compost-filled pots (see page 59).
Swedes	Sow in summer where they are to grow. Thin to 30cm (12in) intervals.
Sweetcorn	Sow under glass in individual pots or modules in spring and plant out in summer at 30cm (12in) intervals, preferably in blocks rather than rows. Can be station sown where they are to grow in early summer.
Swiss chard	Sow in spring where it is to grow and thin to 30cm (12in) intervals.
Thyme	Tip cuttings in spring. It often self-roots, lending it to division in spring. Non-named varieties can also be grown from seed sown in spring or autumn.
Tomatoes	Sow seed under glass in gentle heat in spring. Prick out seedlings and grow on. Transplant outdoor varieties, planting at 60cm (24in) intervals when danger of frost is past. Indoor varieties should be grown in pots or growing bags under cover.
Turnips	Sow from spring onwards for successional crops where they are to grow. Thin to 16cm (6in) apart.
Whitecurrants	Take hardwood cuttings in autumn or winter.

Index

Page numbers in *italics* refer to plants featured in the A–Z propagation directory.

Acknowledgements

BBC Books and OutHouse would like to thank the following for their assistance in preparing this book: Andrew McIndoe for advice and guidance; Robin Whitecross for picture research; Ruth Baldwin for proofreading; Marie Lorimer for the index.

Picture credits

Key t = top, b = bottom, l = left, r = right, c = centre

PHOTOGRAPHS

All photographs by Jonathan Buckley unless listed below.

David Austin Roses 65b

GAP Photos Thomas Alamy 21(1)t; Lee Avison 43(2), 59tc; Pernilla Bergdahl 43(1); Dave Bevan 21(1)b, (2)t & (2)b; Mark Bolton 28bl; Elke Borkowski 53; Keith Burdett 35(3); Victoria Firmston 11, 59l; John Glover 55; Fiona Lea 26t, 41; Clive Nichols 31(3); Sharon Pearson 63; Howard Rice 42t, 57; S & O 31(1); Friedrich Strauss 35(2); Graham Strong 59bc, 65; Visions 31(2); Mark Winwood 30b; Dave Zubraski 40b

Sue Gordon 35(1)

Andrew McIndoe 27t

Marianne Majerus Garden Images 2/3

Robin Whitecross 12, 13, 23b, 34

ILLUSTRATIONS

Lizzie Harper 13, 15, 27, 29, 33, 34, 41, 47t, 54, 57

Sue Hillier 60, 62t & b

Janet Tanner 37, 38, 46, 47b, 48, 49, 51, 55, 61, 64

Thanks are also due to the following designers and owners, whose gardens appear in the book:

Beth Chatto, Beth Chatto Gardens, Essex 39b; Diana Guy, Welcome Thatch, Dorset 14; Carol Klein, Glebe Cottage, Devon 50

While every effort has been made to trace and acknowledge all copyright holders, the publisher would like to apologize should there be any errors or omissions.